ॐ

Sanskrit Samasa Panini Prakriya

Concise and Lucid with Examples

SADHVI HEMSWAROOPA

जय गुरुदेव

ISBN13: 978-93-95766-91-3 Paperback Edition
ISBN13: 978-93-95766-69-2 Hardbound Edition
ISBN13: 978-93-95766-83-8 Digital Edition

Title: **Sanskrit Samasa Panini Prakriya**
SubTitle: Concise and Lucid with Examples
Author: **Sadhvi Hemswaroopa**

Anant Jyot Seva Sansthan
Vadodara 390010
Gujarat, Bhārat

Printed and Published by
Devotees of Sri Sri Ravi Shankar Ashram

Devotees Library Cataloging-in-Publication Data
Hemswaroopa, Sadhvi.
Language: English. Thema: CJBG CJPG 4CTM 2BBA
BISAC: LAN006000 LANGUAGE ARTS & DISCIPLINES / Grammar & Punctuation
Keywords: 1. Sanskrit Grammar. 2. Compound Words. 3. Vyakarana.
Typeset in 12 Source Sans Pro

24th Jan 2024 Punarvasu Nakshatra, Chaturdashi Tithi, Shukla Paksha, Pausha Masa, Shishir Ritu, Uttarayana.

Vikram Samvat 2080 Pingala, Saka Era 1945 Shobhakrit

1st Edition January 2024

जय गुरुदेव

Dedication

H H Sri Sri Ravi Shankar
the Master of KARMA YOGA, DHYANA, JNANA, BHAKTI, BLISS

An offering at His Lotus feet

Blessing

There is that Natural Inquisitiveness, WANTING to KNOW.

Bhakti is not against Knowledge. Lord Krishna says, when there's devotion, it incorporates knowledge within itself.

KNOWLEDGE leads you to DEVOTION, and devotion in turn invokes wisdom from within you.

H H Sri Sri Ravi Shankar
Discourse on Bhagavad Gita 13th Chapter at Bangalore Ashram 13 to 15 Aug 2017

Prayer

ॐ सरस्वति नमस्तुभ्यं वरदे कामरूपिणि । विद्यारंभं करिष्यामि सिद्धिर्भवतु मे सदा ॥

वाक्यकारं वररुचिं भाष्यकारं पतञ्जलिम् । पाणिनिं सूत्रकारञ्च प्रणतोऽस्मि मुनित्रयम् ॥

Table of Contents

The Sanskrit Alphabet

संस्कृत वर्णमाला Sanskrit संस्कृत is written in the देवनागरी Devanagari script, whereas English is written in the Latin (Roman) script.

Conjunct letter संयुक्त अक्षर

क्ष , ज्ञ , श्र are not letters of the alphabet. Rather these are conjuncts that have become popular in writing.

The Sanskrit alphabet is written with or without a halant. Consonants cannot be uttered without a vowel. In teaching, consonants are supplied with vowel अ for uttering.

Here are the 56 letters of the Sanskrit Alphabet.

20 Vowels (ह्रस्व दीर्घ प्लुत short long hail)

अ आ अ३ इ ई इ३ उ ऊ उ३ ऋ ॠ ऋ३ ऌ ऌ३ ए ऐ ए३ ओ औ ओ३

34 Consonants (with halant the half-marker)

क् ख् ग् घ् ङ्

च् छ् ज् झ् ञ्

ट् ठ् ड् ढ् ण्

त् थ् द् ध् न्

प् फ् ब् भ् म्

य् र् ल् व् ळ्

श् ष् स् ह् य्

2 Ayogavahas (Anusvara, Visarga that appear during speaking)

अं अः (ardhavisarga अ×)

Pronunciation of Sanskrit Letters

उच्चारणम्

अ son	आ father	इ it	ई beat	उ full	ऊ pool
ऋ rhythm	ॠ marine	ऌ revelry	ॡ		
ए play	ऐ aisle	ओ go	औ loud		

अं Anusvara is pure nasal – close the lips – similar to म्

अः Visarga is Breath release like ह् and preceding vowel sound

E.g. utter नमः as नमह , शान्तिः as शान्तिहि , विष्णुः as विष्णुहु ।

क seek	ख khan	ग get	घ loghut	ङ sing
च chunk	छ catchhim	ज jump	झ hedgehog	ञ bunch
ट true	ठ anthill	ड drum	ढ godhead	ण under
त tamil	थ thunder	द that	ध breathe	न nut
प put	फ fruit	ब bin	भ abhor	म much
य loyal	र red	ल luck	व vase	
श sure	ष shun	स so	hum ह	

Conjuncts – first utter the top part and then bottom one, e.g.

Bhagavad Gita 10.16 तिष्ठसि → ष्ठ = ष् ठ

Bhagavad Gita 10.23 शङ्करश्चास्मि → ङ्क = ङ्क , श्च = श् च

Specific Conjuncts ह् ण = ह्ण , ह् न = ह्न , ह् म = ह्म

Utter with emphasis on the chest.

2 parameters of Enunciation   Hard consonants are also called surds. व् is a dento-labial
1 उच्चारण स्थानम् Place
ii प्रयत्न   Effort
Place is of 7 different portions in mouth
Effort is of 2 qualities-Tone, amount of breath

	Simple Vowel		1 Hard	2 Hard	3 Soft	4 Soft	⑥ Soft	Soft Semi Vowel	Hard sibilant	Soft
	Short	Long	non-asp	asp	non-asp	asp	nasal			asp
कण्ठ्या: Gutturals ①	अ a	आ ā	क ka	ख kha	ग ga	घ gha	ङ ṅa			ह ha
तालव्या: Palatals ②	इ i	ई ī	च ca	छ cha	ज ja	झ jha	ञ ña	य ya	श śa	
मूर्धन्या: retroflex Cerebrals or Linguals ③	ऋ ṛ (अ+र्)	ॠ ṝ	ट ṭa	ठ ṭha	ड ḍa	ढ ḍha	ण ṇa	र ra	ष ṣa	
दन्त्या: Dentals ④	ऌ ḷ (अ+ल्)		त ta	थ tha	द da	ध dha	न na	ल la	स sa	
ओष्ठ्या: Labials ⑤	उ u	ऊ ū	प pa	फ pha	ब ba	भ bha	म ma	व va dento labial		ᳵ

a) Short vowel··· अ इ उ ऋ ऌ

b) Long vowel···· आ ई ऊ ॠ

① Visarga is guttural
the ⑤ upadhmaniya is ~~guttural~~labial 7) The jihvamuliya is spoken from root of tongue

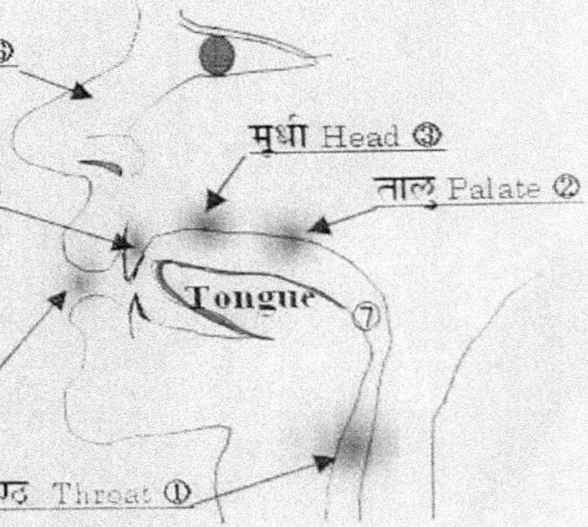

4) Compound Vowel or Diphthongs {एच्}

कण्ठ-तालु Gutturo-palatals	ए e	ऐ ai
कण्ठ-ओष्ठ्यम् Gutturo-labials	ओ o	औ au

5) व दन्त-ओष्ठ्यम् dento labial   6) ं anusvara is nasal नासिका

Saraswati Puja

Saraswati Puja for good education. We all chanted ॐ ऐं ह्रीं सरस्वत्यै नमः Om Aim Hrim Sarasvatyae Namah during Navratri Navami 3pm 13Oct2013. Course books for dissemination to each pupil being blessed.

Structure of the Sanskrit Language

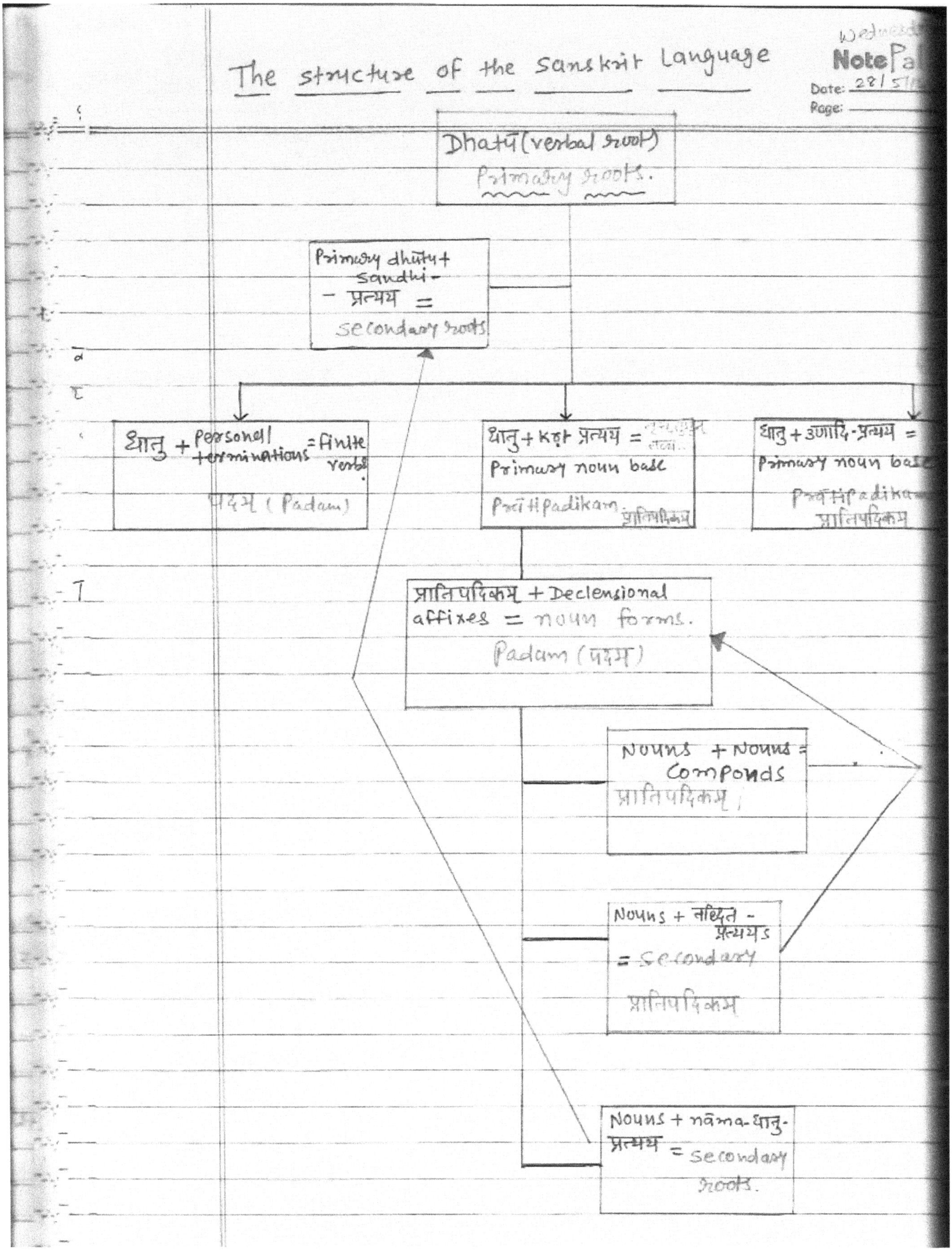

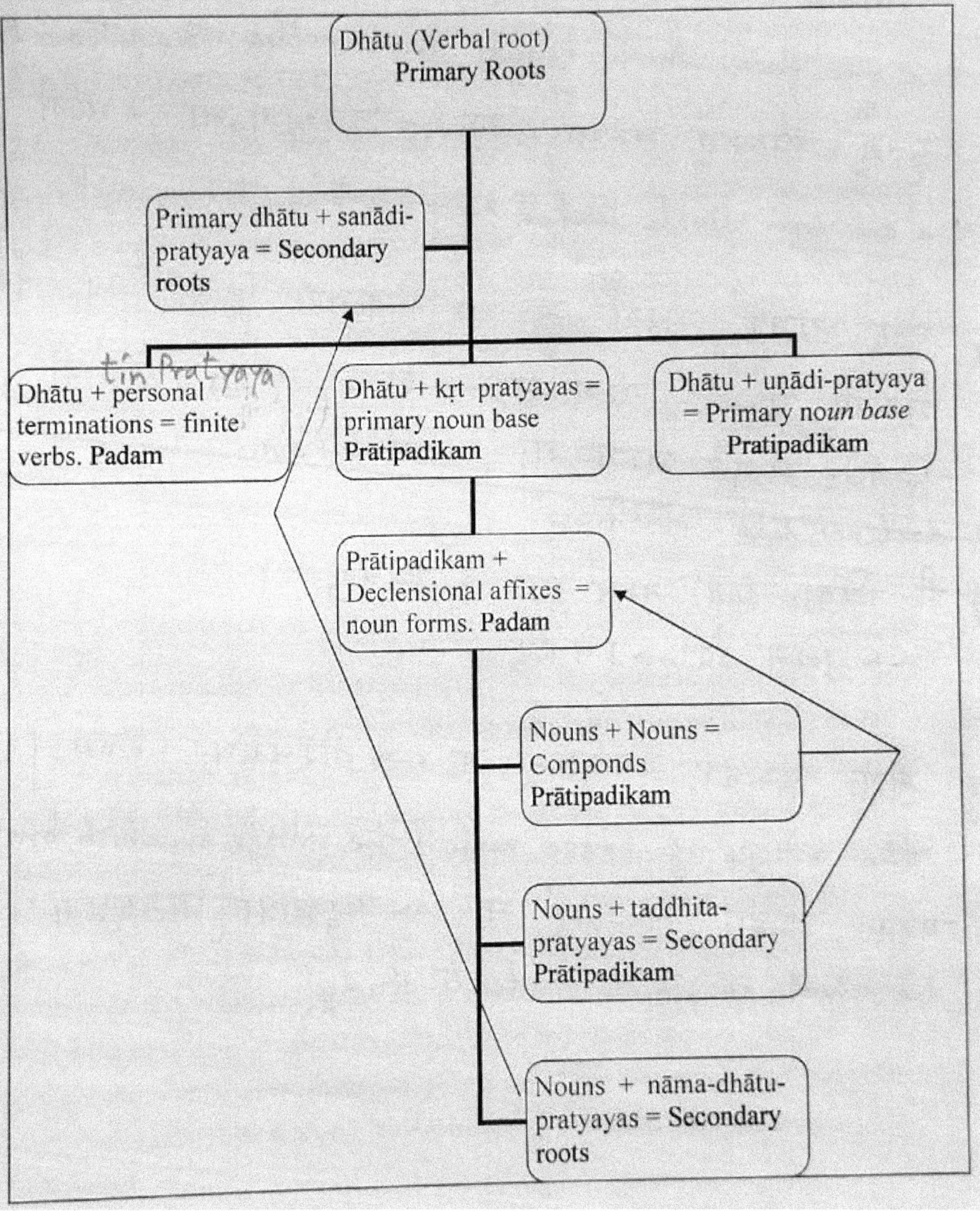
Dhātu (Verbal root)
Primary Roots
Primary dhātu + sanādi-pratyaya = Secondary roots
tin Pratyaya
Dhātu + personal terminations = finite verbs. Padam
Dhātu + kṛt pratyayas = primary noun base Prātipadikam
Dhātu + uṇādi-pratyaya = Primary noun base Pratipadikam
Prātipadikam + Declensional affixes = noun forms. Padam
Nouns + Nouns = Componds Prātipadikam
Nouns + taddhita-pratyayas = Secondary Prātipadikam
Nouns + nāma-dhātu-pratyayas = Secondary roots

Samasa Notes Jan to March 2014

Compound words are frequently seen in Sanskrit Vedanta and Upanishad texts. These are condensed sentences, nay entire paragraphs of subtle wisdom.

2.1.4 सह सुपा । With a word ending in a case-affix.
In this sutra the word अय is implicit, so it consists of three words, सुप् सह सुपा ।

1. सह सुप् समस्यते समर्थेन a case-inflected word may be compounded with a word with which it is connected in sense. To put it another way, a join of two words that are somehow meaningfully related.

2. सुपा सह समस्यते a case-inflected word is compounded with another sup-inflected word, i.e. compounding a tinganta/subanta pada with a subantam padam.

Definition of Samasa = Compound Word

समासः Compound.

Tuesday. 9:15 Am.
Page No. 23
Date 21 / 1 / 14

When 2 सुबन्तं पदम्s which are meaningfully connected in a such a way that, they can be combined to give a unified meaning, are combined it is called the process of compounding = समासः। = समसनम् । (समसन-ग्)

The combined word is also called a समासः। = that which is combined (कर्म-व्युत्पत्तिः)

Broadly there are 4 types of समासः।

1) अव्ययीभावः। - पूर्वपदप्रधानः - The 1st word is important.

2) तत्पुरुषः। - उत्तरपदप्रधानः - The 2nd word (later word) is important.
The compound represents (denotes) the 2nd word.

3) बहुव्रीहिः। - अन्यपदप्रधानः - A compound denotes a word external to the compound.

4) द्वन्द्वः। - सर्वपदप्रधानः - All the words are equally (denoted) important.

In अव्ययीभावः and तत्पुरुषः only 2 words can combine at a time to form a compound.

In बहुव्रीहिः- and द्वन्द्वः more than 2 words can combine at a time.

But we do not see more than 3 words forming a बहुव्रीहिः. On the otherhand (any) 'n' - number of words can combine to form a द्वन्द्वः।.

- Compounded words - समस्तपदम् ।

non compounded words - व्यस्तपदम् ।, असमस्त पदम् ।

1) समसनं समासः । Putting two or more words together into one word is called समासः।

Ex: दशरथस्य पुत्रः → दशरथपुत्रः।
सीतायाः पतिः → सीतापतिः।

2) समासः सुबन्तानां = पदानां भवति न तु तिङन्तानां = पदानाम् ।

3) समासः युगपत् (at a time/once) द्वयोः = द्वयोः = सुबन्तयोः भवति । द्वन्द्वे तु बहूनाम् अपि।

Ex: (a) राज्ञः पुरुषः —GTP→ राजपुरुषः → राजपुरुषस्य आगमनम् → राजपुरुषागमनम्

(b) रामस्य आगमनम् —GTP→ रामागमनम्
रामागमनस्य वार्ता —GTP→ रामागमनवार्ता
रामागमनवार्तायाः श्रवणम् —GTP→ रामागमनवार्ताश्रवणम् ।
– रामागमनवार्ताश्रवणेन भरतः तुष्यति ।

(c) In case of द्वन्द्व – [बहूनां = सुबन्तानां = पदानां युगपत् समासः भवति]

रामः च कृष्णः च हरिः च —द्वन्द्वः→ रामकृष्णहरयः ।
रामः च लक्ष्मणः च भरतः च शत्रुघ्नः च द्वन्द्व रामलक्ष्मणभरतशत्रुघ्नाः

4) परस्परान्वितयोः = सुबन्तयोः समासः भवति ।
(परस्परम् अन्वितम् - कर्मधारय समास)

Two mutually connected सुबन्तम् पदम्s alone will form a compound. The mutual connection should be meaningful connection.

(a) भवति दर्शनं राज्ञः पुरुषः अमात्यस्य धावति ।

(b) पश्य भार्या राज्ञः पुरुषः देवदत्तस्य स्तः ।

Here शत्रोः and पुरुषः are not mutually meaningfully connected therefore, they can not a combined to form a समासः।

A समास can be made only between two words which are meaningfully connected through a कारक.

In these two examples the शत्रोः and पुरुषः are not connected meaningfully therefore, a compound can not be made. (शत्रो = प्रा. शमन + कर्म)

5) समासे पूर्वं श्रूयमाणं पदं पूर्वपदम्। उत्तरम् श्रूयमाणं पदम् उत्तरपदम्।

In the समास the word which is heard first is called पूर्वपदम् and the word which is heard after (last) is called उत्तरपदम्।

Ex: चोरात् भयम् —5 TP→ चोरभयम्।
पूर्वपदम् उत्तरपदम्

There are definite rule as to which will be the पूर्वपदम् in any compound. Those we will see later with सूत्रs.

6) The Process of Compounding:

1. The words should be meaningfully connected.
2. That meaningful connection (the कारक connection) should be compoundable by the rules of grammar.
3. The two words compounded are पदम्s and as it is they are, in a sentence and form the sentence they are taken up for compounding.

Ex: दशरथस्य पुत्रः = रामः वनं गतवान्।

Two Principle Types of Samasa = KevalSamasa and VisheshaSamasa

Friday 24/1/14

दशरथस्य पुत्रः षष्ठी तत्पुरुषः → दशरथ + ङस् + पुत्र + सु

लौकिक-विग्रहवाक्यम्। अलौकिक-विग्रह-वाक्यम् →

case affixes drop → दशरथपुत्र + सु → दशरथपुत्रः

प्रातिपदिकम् प्रत्यय समस्त पदम् (समास)

- दशरथपुत्रः रामः वनं गतवान्।
- → दशरथस्य पुत्रेण रावणः हतः।
  दशरथपुत्रेण रावणः हतः।
- → दशरथस्य पुत्रं हनुमान् पश्यति।
  दशरथपुत्रं हनुमान् पश्यति।

Friday 24/1/14 9:15 AM

समासः द्विविधः

(1) केवलसमासः

(2) विशेषसमासः

(1) अव्ययीभावः।
(2) तत्पुरुषः।
(3) बहुव्रीहिः।
(4) द्वन्द्वः।

(2) तत्पुरुषः समासः।

तत्पुरुषः समासः is of four types: (1) सामान्यः 7
(2) कर्मधारयः 8
(3) द्विगुः 3
(4) नञ्-प्रभृतयः 5
नञ् तत्पुरुष etc

KevalSamasa means simply a compound of two joined words. VisheshaSamasa means a compound word having a specific intrinsic meaning, that can be much larger than its consituent words.

4 Types of VisheshaSamasa= AvyayiBhava TatPurusha Bahuvrihi Dvandva

The VisheshaSamasa compound word has the four major types.

- I. TatPurusha, i.e. ThatBeing
- II. Bahuvrihi, i.e. ManyTypes/Indeterminate
- III. Dvandva, i.e. Noun word joins having equal or similar importance
- IV. AvyayiBhava, i.e. that which is an Indeclinable

4 Types of TatPurusha Samasa = Samanya Karmadharya Dvigu Nan

The TatPurusha compound word has the four major types.

- Samanya TatPurusha, i.e. the general ThatBeing, 2.1.24 द्वितीया श्रितातीतपतितगतात्यस्तप्राप्तापन्नैः
- Karmadharya TatPurusha, i.e. the action oriented ThatBeing
- Dvigu TatPurusha, i.e. having a numeric meaning, 2.1.23 द्विगुश्च
- Nan TatPurusha, i.e. Complementary or Anti

There are 7 subTypes of Samanya TatPurusha Samasa
There are 8 subTypes of Karmadharya TatPurusha Samasa
There are 3 subTypes of Dvigu TatPurusha Samasa
There are 5 subTypes of Nan TatPurusha Samasa

A. Vishesha Samasa = Special/Specific Compounds

Many compounds are seen in the Vedic literature, viz. the Upanishad texts etc., and also in the Classical literature, eg. The Bhagavad Gita and the epics, the Ramayana and the Mahabharata, etc.

These compound words are not simply joins of two words. Rather many have a much greater and profound intrinsic meaning, that is beautiful and mesmerising at the same time.

I. TatPurusha Samasa = Determinative Compound

2.1.22 तत्पुरुषः । ThatBeing or TatPurusha compound is so named, since the sense of the last of its words is the main one, and governs the preceding one.

2.1.50 दिक्संख्ये संज्ञायाम् ।

2.1.51 तद्धितार्थोत्तरपदसमाहारे च । In a case where the sense is that of

- a Tadddhita affix or
- when an additional member comes after the compound or
- when an aggregate is to be expressed,

then a word signifying a point of the compass or a number (2.1.50), enters into composition with a case-inflected word which is in agreement with it by being in the same case, and the resulting compound is a TatPurusha compound.

Samanya TatPurusha = General

A word ending in Agent 1st case affix compounded with another case inflected word results in a TatPurusha compound. 2.2.1 पूर्वापराधरोत्तरमेकदेशिनैकाधिकरणे ।

Page No. 27

1) प्रथमा तत्पुरुषः।

A. When there is a relationship of a 'part' to the 'whole', there the word denoting the part joins with the word denoting the 'whole' and becomes a तत्पुरुष समास ।

Words denoting the part (अवयव) that can combine are only.

पूर्व - before / front, अपर - other, अधर - below / lower, उत्तर above / upper. and अर्ध (n) half,

The words denoting the 'whole' can be anything.

अर्ध ग्रामस्य —प्र. तत्पु.→ अर्ध + सु + ग्राम + ङस् —drop case→ अर्धग्राम —परवत् लिङ्ग→ अर्धग्रामः ।

पूर्वपद उत्तरपद

Half of a village.

(*) Note: In any द्वन्द्वः or तत्पुरुष compound the gender of the compounded is similar to that of the last word. The समास denotes the last words :— उत्तरपद प्रधानः तत्पुरुषः ।

Ex: नृपः ग्रामस्य अर्धं आचार्याय ददाति ।

नृपः अर्धग्रामम् आचार्याय ददाति ।

पूर्वं कायस्य - पूर्वकायः । - lower part of the body.

अपरं भवनस्य - अपरभवनम् । - lower part of the building.

अधरं गृहस्य - अधरगृहम् । - lower part of the house.

उत्तरं रात्रेः - उत्तररात्रः । -

Note: There is a rule that the word रात्रि (f) will become रात्र and masculine if it is end of a समासः ।

Page No. 23

B. All words denoting part (एकदेश) will combine with a word denoting time to form (प्रथमा) तत्पुरुषः।

अहन् = day (m) अह्नः (6/1) [In a compound अहन् is replaced by अह्न]

- मध्यम् (1/1 N) अह्नः (6/1) —तत्पु.→ मध्य + सु (1/1) + अहन् + ङस् (6/1) → मध्य + अह्न —दीर्घसन्धिः→ मध्याह्न (m) —परवत् लिङ्ग→ मध्याह्नः। Noon.

- पूर्वम् (1/1 N) अह्नः (6/1) → पूर्वाह्नः —णत्वम्→ पूर्वाह्णः। fore noon

- अपरम् (1/1 N) अह्नः (6/1) → अपराह्नः —णत्वम्→ अपराह्णः। after noon.

- मध्यम् (1/1) रात्रेः (6/1) → मध्यरात्रः। midnight

- सायम् अह्नः (6/1) → सायाह्नः। evening

Monday 9.15

2.1.24 द्वितीया श्रितातीतपतितगतात्यस्तप्राप्तापन्नैः । A word ending in Accusative 2nd case affix is compounded with the words श्रित *the one dependent upon*, अतीत *the one gone forth*, पतित *the one who is fallen*, गत *the one who has gone*, अत्यस्त *the one who has left*, प्राप्त *the one who has attained* and अपान्न *the one who has reached*, then the resulting word is a TatPurusha compound.

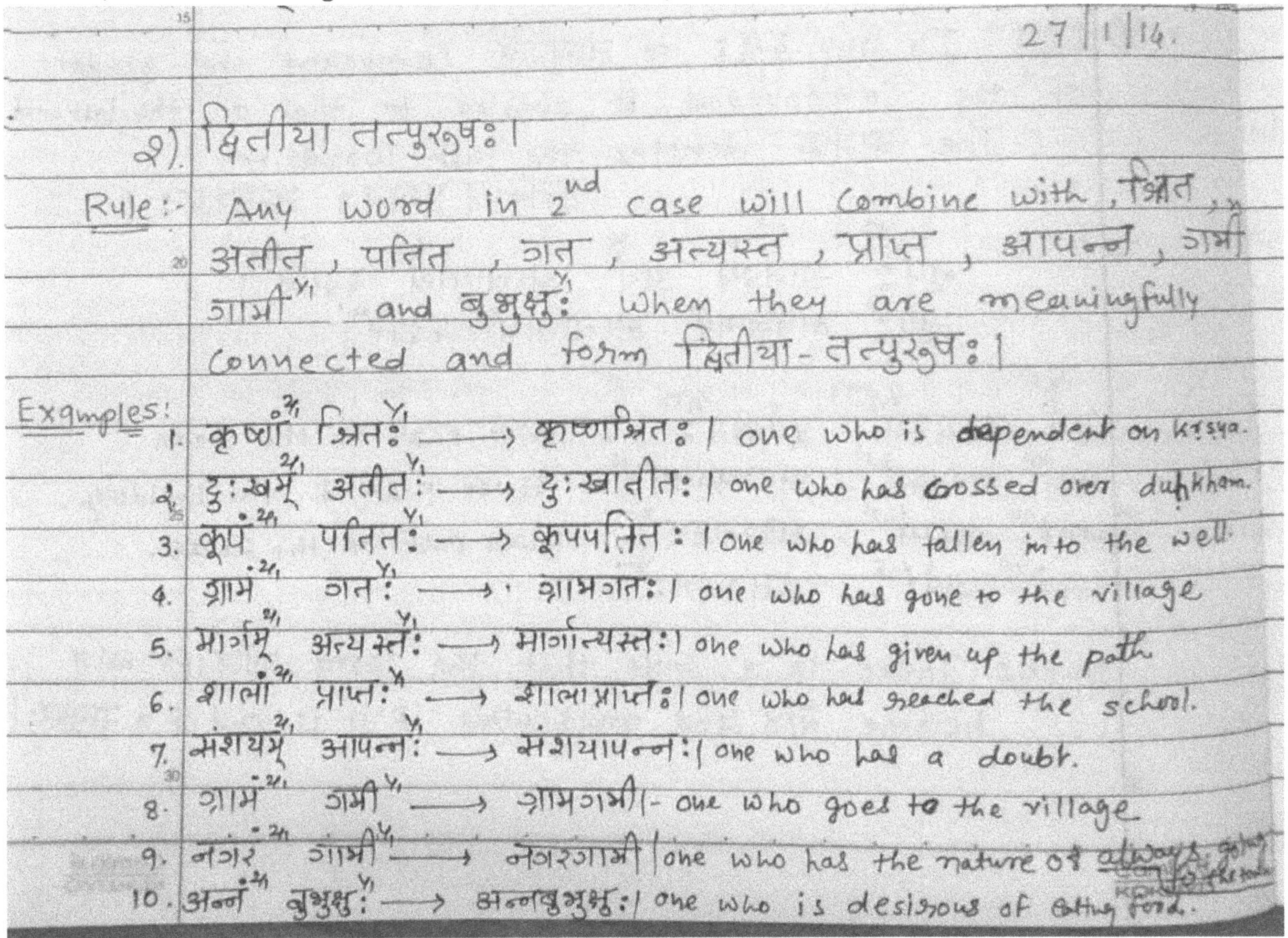

27/1/14.

2) द्वितीया तत्पुरुषः।

Rule:- Any word in 2nd case will combine with, श्रित, अतीत, पतित, गत, अत्यस्त, प्राप्त, आपन्न, गामी, गामी and बुभुक्षुः when they are meaningfully connected and form द्वितीया-तत्पुरुषः।

Examples:

1. कृष्णं श्रितः → कृष्णश्रितः। one who is dependent on Krṣṇa.
2. दुःखम् अतीतः → दुःखातीतः। one who has crossed over duḥkham.
3. कूपं पतितः → कूपपतितः। one who has fallen into the well.
4. ग्रामं गतः → ग्रामगतः। one who has gone to the village
5. मार्गम् अत्यस्तः → मार्गात्यस्तः। one who has given up the path
6. शालां प्राप्तः → शालाप्राप्तः। one who has reached the school.
7. संशयम् आपन्नः → संशयापन्नः। one who has a doubt.
8. ग्रामं गामी → ग्रामगामी। - one who goes to the village
9. नगरं गामी → नगरगामी। one who has the nature of always going to the town
10. अन्नं बुभुक्षुः → अन्नबुभुक्षुः। one who is desirous of eating food.

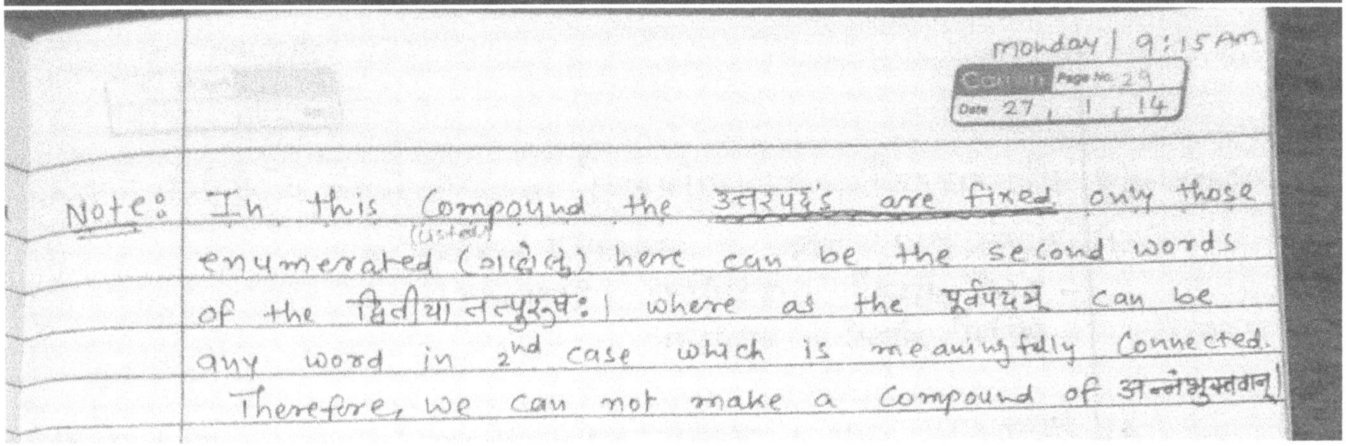

Monday | 9:15 AM

Page No. 29

Date 27 / 1 / 14

Note: In this compound the उत्तरपद's are fixed only those enumerated (listed) here can be the second words of the द्वितीया तत्पुरुषः। where as the पूर्वपदम् can be any word in 2nd case which is meaningfully connected.

Therefore, we can not make a compound of अन्नंभुक्तवान्।

2.1.30 तृतीया तत्कृतार्थेन गुणवचनेन । A word ending in Instrumental 3rd case affix is compounded with तत्कृतार्थेन *what denotes quality*, गुणवचनेन *the quality being that which is* caused by a word ending in Instrumental 3rd case affix, and with the word अर्थ *wealth*, then the resulting word is a TatPurusha compound.

2.1.31 पूर्वसदृशसमोनार्थकलहनिपुणमिश्रश्लक्ष्णैः । A word ending in Instrumental 3rd case affix is compounded with the words पूर्व *prior*, सदृश *like*, सम *similar*, अनर्थ *having the sense of less*, कलह *quarrel*, निपुण *proficient*, मिश्र *mixed* and श्लक्षण *polished*, then the resulting word is a TatPurusha compound.

2.1.32 कर्तृकरणे कृता बहुलम् । A word ending in Instrumental 3rd case affix when it denotes the कर्तृ *agent* or करणे *instrument*, is compounded बहुलम् *diversely* with what ends with a कृत् affix, then the resulting word is a TatPurusha compound.

2.1.33 कृत्यैरधिकार्थवचने । A word ending in Instrumental 3rd case affix when it denotes the कर्तृ *agent* or करणे *instrument*, is compounded with a word ending in a कृत्य affix, when an अधिक-अर्थ-वचने *exaggeration whether of praise or of censure is implied*, then the resulting word is a TatPurusha compound.

2.1.34 अन्नेन व्यञ्जनम् । A word ending in Instrumental 3rd case affix denoting व्यञ्जनम् *a condiment*, is compounded with a word signifying व्यञ्जनम् *a condiment item*, then the resulting word is a TatPurusha compound.

2.1.35 भक्ष्येण मिश्रीकरणम् । A word ending in Instrumental 3rd case affix denoting मिश्रीकरणम् *delicious*, is compounded with a word signifying भक्ष्येण *eatables*, then the resulting word is a TatPurusha compound.

3) तृतीयातत्पुरुषः । -

Rule:1 A word in 3rd case meaningfully connected to the following words combines with them to form तृतीयातत्पुरुषः।

Note: Here also the उत्तरपद's are fixed and पूर्वपद's are open. The उत्तरपद's here are पूर्व, सदृश, सम, ऊनार्थ, कलह, निपुण, मिश्र, संमिश्र, श्लक्ष्ण, and अवर। (these all are प्रातिपदिका's)
ऊनार्थ - is a group of words having the meaning of 'less'.

Examples:

1. मासेन(3/1) पूर्वः(1/1) = मासपूर्वः। - prior by a month.
2. मात्रा(3/1) सदृशः(1/1) = मातृसदृशः। - Like the mother.
3. पित्रा(3/1) समः(1/1) = पितृसमः। - Like the father.
4. कार्षापणेन(3/1) ऊनम् = कार्षापणोनम्। - Less by one कार्षापण (quarter.)
   कार्षापणेन विकलम् = कार्षापणविकलम् - Less by one "
   [ऊन = विकल = less = ऊनार्थ - शब्दौ]
5. वाचा(3/1) कलहः ⟹ वाक्कलहः।
   प्रा. → वाच् वाचा(3/1) कलहः(1/1) = वाच् + टा(3/1) (आ) + कलह + सु → वाच् + कलह —चो: कुः / कुत्वम्→ वाक्कलह → वाक्कलहः।
   पदम् (at the end of the पद a इत्त follows.)
6. आचारेण(3/1) निपुणः(1/1) = आचारनिपुणः(1/1) He expert because of conduct.
7. गुडेन(3/1) मिश्रः(1/1) = गुडमिश्रः(1/1) mixed with jagry.
8. आचारेण(3/1) श्लक्ष्णः(1/1) = आचारश्लक्ष्णः(1/1) he is proper due to his good conduct.
9. मासेन(3/1) अवरः(1/1) = मासावरः(1/1)। lesser by a month.

Tuesday. 19:15 Am

Comlin Page No. 30

Date 28 / 1 / 14

· Rule no. 2 संस्कारद्रव्य (3/1) + अन्नवाचिशब्दः (1/1) → will form a तृतीया- तत्पुरुषः

1) संस्कारद्रव्य = दधि , अन्नवाचि = ओदन

- दध्ना (3/1) ओदनः (1/1) = दध्योदनः (दध्यन्नम्)

- क्षीरेण (3/1) ओदनः (1/1) = क्षीरोदनः

2) मिश्रीकरणम् with a भक्ष्यम् (sss ...) eg. hard food, crunchy food).

गुडेन (3/1) पृथुकाः (1/3 m) → गुडपृथुकाः (1/1 m.) (पोह्या ...)

गुडेन (3/1) धानाः → गुडधानाः (1/1)

Rule no: 3. (Imp.)

Any word in 3rd case denoting agent (कर्ता) or instrument (करणम्) will combine with a meaningfully related कृदन्तपदम् and form a तृतीया- तत्पुरुषः।

That is कर्तरि- तृतीया and करणे- तृतीया will combine with a related कृदन्तपदम्।

Examples:

हरिणा (3/1) त्रातः (1/1) = हरित्रातः (1/1)। कर्तरि तृतीया Protected by हरि / Passive.

तेन (3/1) कृतम् (1/1) = तत्कृतम् (1/1)। "

कालिदासेन (3/1) रचितम् (1/1) = कालिदासरचितम् (1/1)। " "

- परशुना (3/1) विच्छिन्नम् = परशुविच्छिन्नम् (1/1)। करणे तृतीया by the axe it was broken.

नखैः भिन्नः = नखभिन्नः। " "

खड्गेन (3/1) छिन्नः = खड्गछिन्नः।

Note: In this rule there is no restriction (नियंत्रण) on the first word and the second word but in the सूत्र, there is a word. बहुलम्। Because of that word. Some words that are not intended (हेतुपूर्वक) are also included (समावेश) and will get compound or

Some words which could get compound by this सूत्र will not be compounded.

* दण्डेन[3/1] ताडितवान्[1/1] will not combine to form a तृतीया-तत्पुरुषः

- That is any करणे-तृतीया will not combine with any कर्तरिकृदन्त.

Here the word दण्डेन is करणे-तृतीया and ताडितवान् is कर्तरिकृदन्त that's why it will not combine as a compound.

Like: ex

1) हस्तेन खादितवान् ।

2) पादेन चलितवान् ।

2.1.36 **चतुर्थी तदर्थार्थबलिहितसुखरक्षितैः ।** A word ending in Dative 4th case affix is compounded with the word **तदर्थ** *denoting that which is for the purpose of* in Dative 4th case, and with the words **अर्थ** *on account of*, **बलि** *a sacrifice*, **हित** *salutary*, **सुख** *pleasure* and **रक्षित** *kept*, then the resulting word is a TatPurusha compound.

4) चतुर्थी- तत्पुरुषः ।

Rule: 1

The तादर्थ्य-चतुर्थी will combine to form a चतुर्थी-तत्पुरुष. when there is a प्रकृति (कारण) - विकृति (कार्य) भाव सम्बन्ध is there between the two words.

Examples:

कुण्डलाय हिरण्यम् → कुण्डलहिरण्यम् ।

यूपाय दारु → यूपदारु ।

Here the हिरण्यम् and दारु are प्रकृति-s (कारण) the कुण्डल and यूप are विकृति-s (कार्य)

And there is तादर्थ्यचतुर्थी connection between them. Therefore, compounding takes place. (यूप = secrificial post)

नैवेद्य / निवेद्य offering

Rule: 2

The तादर्थ्यचतुर्थी will combine with हित, बलि, सुख and रक्षित when they are meaningfully connected to form a चतुर्थी- तत्पुरुषः ।

Examples:

भूतेभ्यः बलिः = भूतबलिः ।

भूतेभ्यः हितम् = भूतहितम् ।

गवे हितम् = गोहितम् ।

गवे सुखम् = गोसुखम् ।

गवे रक्षितम् = गोरक्षितम् । Some thing that is preserved for the cow

Rule : 3 The तादर्थ्यचतुर्थी will combine with the word अर्थ, as a नित्यसमास and form a चतुर्थीतत्पुरुष. And here the word अर्थ itself also has the meaning of प्रयोजनम् ('for the sake of'). And eventhough this is a तत्पुरुष, the compound is an adjective to an external word and therefore, can be used all the three genders.

Example: नित्यसमास -

ब्राह्मणाय अयम् → ब्राह्मणार्थः सूपः

छात्राय इयम् यवागूः → छात्रार्था यवागूः

बालाय इदम् पयः → बालार्थं पयः।

Note: Here the sentence where the compound takes place is ब्राह्मणाय अयम् सूपः।

The compounding is taking place between ब्राह्मणाय & अयम् but the अयम् is not included in compound and the second word brought is 'अर्थ' which has the meaning of the प्रयोजनम् or purpose and compounding takes place as follows.

ब्राह्मणाय अयम् सूपः → ब्राह्मणाय अर्थः। →

= ब्राह्मण + ङे + अर्थ + सु

= ब्राह्मणार्थ

विशेष्यलिङ्गः therefore ब्राह्मणार्थः सूपः।

It is called नित्यसमास because the word अर्थ is seen only in the compound and not in the विग्रहवाक्य. That is the word अर्थ is permanently compounded to a word in a 4th case in the sense of 'for the sake of'.

Because it is permanently compounded

Thursday | 3:30 pm.
Page No. 33
Date 30 , 1 , 14

in this ~~(matter)~~ manner. it is called नित्यसमास।
and the समास /compound it self is an adjective
to an outsides word, as can be seen in the Examples.

* This चतुर्थी तत्पुरुष compounds ending in अर्थ can be use as क्रियाविशेषणम् /adverb.. such use is very common.

Example:

भोजनार्थं$^{2/1}$ भोजनशालां$^{2/1}$ गच्छति$^{III/1}$। for the sake of eating.

adverb | क्रियाविशेषण

पठनार्थं$^{2/1}$ पाठशालां$^{2/1}$ गच्छन्ति$^{III/3}$। for the sake of studying.

2.1.37 पञ्चमी भयेन । A word ending in Ablative 5th case affix is compounded with the word भय *fear*, then the resulting word is a TatPurusha compound.

2.1.38 अपेतापोढमुक्तपतितापत्रस्तैरल्पशः । A word ending in Ablative 5th case affix is compounded with the words अपेत *gone away*, अपोध *carried away*, मुक्त *freed*, पतित *fallen*, अपत्रस्त *afraid of*, when the event takes place in a gradual manner, then the resulting word is a TatPurusha compound.

2.1.39 स्तोकान्तिकदूरार्थकृच्छ्राणि क्तेन । When words with a sense of स्तोक *little*, अन्तिक *near*, दूर *far* and कृच्छ्र *penance*, ending in Ablative 5th case affix, are compounded with what ends in क्त affix, then the resulting word is a TatPurusha compound.

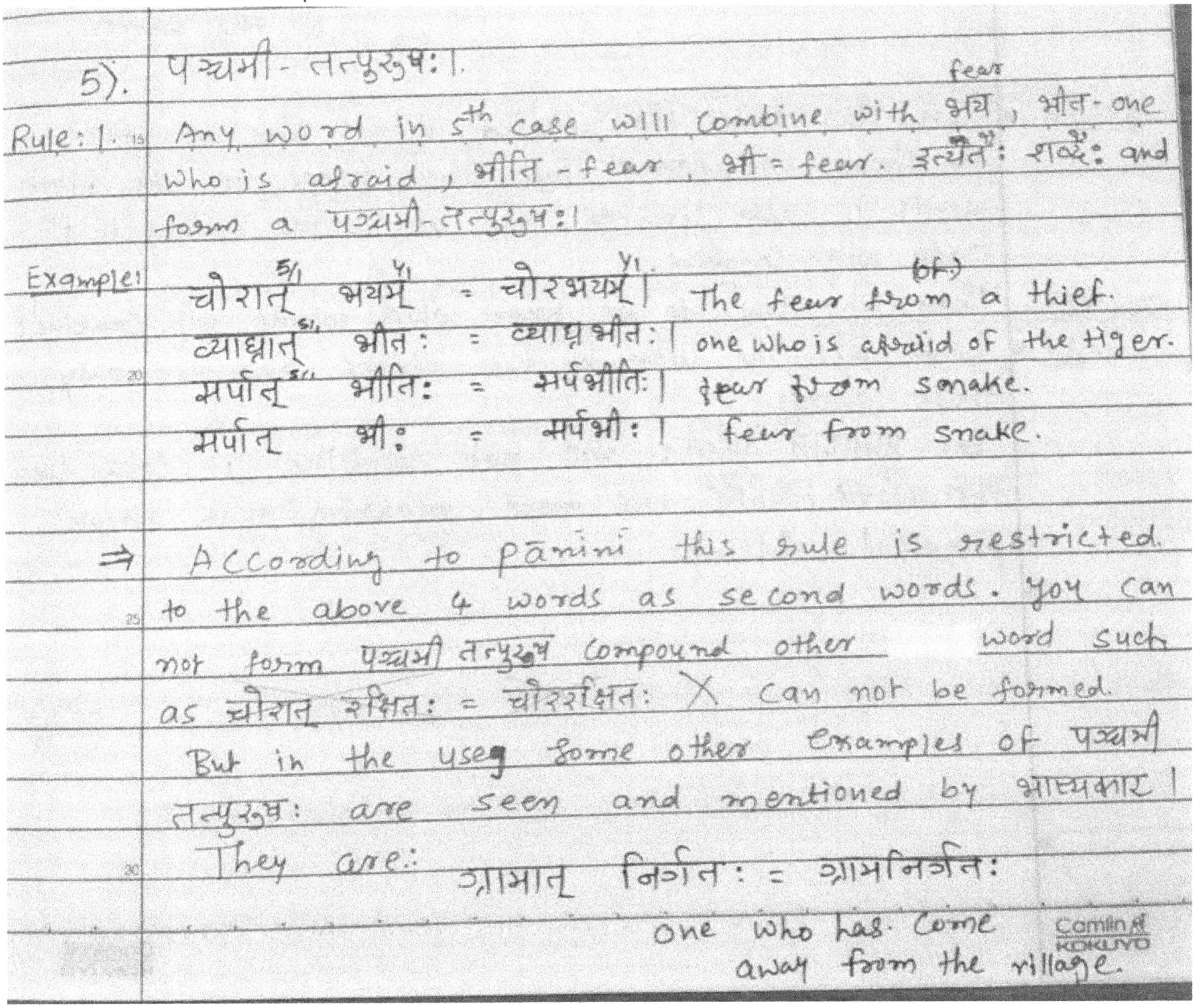
5). पञ्चमी- तत्पुरुषः।

Rule: 1. Any word in 5th case will combine with भय (fear), भीत- one who is afraid, भीति - fear, भी = fear. इत्येतैः शब्दैः and form a पञ्चमी-तत्पुरुषः।

Example:
चौरात् (5/1) भयम् (1/1) = चौरभयम् (1/1)। The fear (of) from a thief.
व्याघ्रात् (5/1) भीतः = व्याघ्रभीतः। one who is afraid of the tiger.
सर्पात् (5/1) भीतिः = सर्पभीतिः। fear from snake.
सर्पात् भीः = सर्पभीः। fear from snake.

⇒ According to pāṇini this rule is restricted to the above 4 words as second words. You can not form पञ्चमी तत्पुरुष compound other word such as चौरात् रक्षितः = चौररक्षितः ✗ can not be formed.
But in the useg some other examples of पञ्चमी तत्पुरुषः are seen and mentioned by भाष्यकार।
They are: ग्रामात् निर्गतः = ग्रामनिर्गतः
one who has come away from the village.

Camlin Page No. 34

अधर्मात् जुगुप्सुः = अधर्मजुगुप्सुः। one who refrains from

Rule: 2 · Some word in 5th case will combine with अपेत - अपोढ - मुक्त - पतित - अपत्रस्त - शब्दैः to form पञ्चमी तत्पुरुषः।

Examples:

सुखात् [5/1] अपेतः [1/1]। = सुखापेतः। one who has moved away from सुखम्

कल्पनायाः अपोढः। = कल्पनापोढः। one who has moved away from imagination

चक्राद् [5/1] मुक्तः। = चक्रमुक्तः। one who has been freed from the wheel.

स्वर्गात् [5/1] पतितः। = स्वर्गपतितः। one who has fallen from स्वर्ग

तरङ्गात् [5/1] अपत्रस्तः। = तरङ्गापत्रस्तः। one who has been thrown of the waves.

Notes: In this rule the second words are all fixed to those mentioned. But the scope of the first word is also limited. not all words ending in 5th case will combine.

Que: Than How do we know which words will Combine?

Ans: Look for the useg by the elders and use only those words.

Ex: प्रासादात् पतितः will not Combine it looks like the word पतित has more meaning than simple physical falling.

2.2.8 षष्ठी । A word ending in Genetive 6th case affix is compounded with a case inflected word, then the resulting word is a TatPurusha compound.

6) षष्ठी - तत्पुरुषः।

Any word in 6th case will combine with a meaningfully related word to form a षष्ठी-तत्पुरुषः।

Examples:

राज्ञः$^{6/1}$ पुरुषः$^{1/1}$ = राजपुरुषः।

दशरथस्य$^{6/1}$ पुत्रः$^{1/1}$ = दशरथपुत्रः।

विद्यायाः$^{6/1}$ आलयः$^{1/1}$ = विद्यालयः।

मम$^{6/1}$ आचार्यः$^{1/1}$ = मदाचार्यः।

अस्माकं आचार्यः = अस्मदाचार्यः।

तव पादम् = त्वत्पादम्।

युष्माकं पुस्तकानि = युष्मत्पुस्तकानि।

* अस्मत् + युष्मत् replaced by मत् and त्वत् when compounded in the singular only.

Singular: मम$^{6/1}$ आचार्यः$^{1/1}$ —GTP→ अस्मत् + ङस् + आचार्य + सुँ

अस्मत् → [मत्] + आचार्य —जश्→ मदाचार्य → मदाचार्यः।

replaced by मत् because it is singular.

Plural: अस्माकम्$^{6/3}$ आचार्यः$^{1/1}$ —GTP→ अस्मत् + ङस् + आचार्य + सुँ

→ अस्मत् + आचार्य —जश्→ अस्मदाचार्य → अस्मदाचार्यः।

तव$^{6/1}$ पादम्$^{1/1}$ → युष्मत् + ङस् + पाद + सुँ —

युष्मत् replaced by त्वत् ∵ it is singular → त्वत् + पाद —जश्→ त्वद् पाद —चर्→ त्वत् पाद → त्वत्पाद → त्वत्पादम्

Aside Rule: When the प्रातिपदिकाs अस्मत् and युष्मत् are the first word in a compound, if they are singular, they are replaced by मत् and त्वत् respectively.

2.1.40 सप्तमी शौण्डैः । A word ending in Locative 7th case affix is compounded with the words शौण्ड *skilled* etc., then the resulting word is a TatPurusha compound.

2.1.41 सिद्धशुष्कपक्वबन्धैश्च । A word ending in Locative 7th case affix is compounded with the words सिद्ध *perfected*, शुष्क *dried*, पक्व *cooked*, and बन्ध *bound*, then the resulting word is a TatPurusha compound.

2.1.42 ध्वाङ्क्षेण क्षेपे । A word ending in Locative 7th case affix is compounded with the word ध्वाङ्क्ष *crow* and synonyms of crow when क्षेपे *contempt* is implied, then the resulting word is a TatPurusha compound.

2.1.43 कृत्यैर्ऋणे । A word ending in Locative 7th case affix is compounded with words ending with कृत्य affix (Future Passive Participle), then the resulting word is a TatPurusha compound.

2.1.44 संज्ञायाम् । A word ending in Locative 7th case affix is compounded with a word ending in a case-affix, when the compound thus formed is used as an appellative/definition/name, then the resulting word is a TatPurusha compound.

2.1.45 क्तेनाहोरात्रावयवाः । When the names of divisions of day or night ending with Locative 7th case affix are compounded with words ending with क्त affix, then the resulting word is a TatPurusha compound.

2.1.46 तत्र । When the word तत्र *there,* which is a word ending with Locative 7th case affix is compounded with words ending with क्त affix, then the resulting word is a TatPurusha compound.

2.1.47 क्षेपे । When a word ending in Locative 7th case affix is compounded with words ending with क्त affix when क्षेपे *censure* is implied, then the resulting word is a TatPurusha compound.

2.1.48 पात्रेसमितादयश्च ।

7) सप्तमी-तत्पुरुषः।

q. Any word in 7th case will combine with,

crook. → धूर्त - शौण्ड - कितव -,

expert → प्रवीण - पण्डित - कुशल - निपुण -,

- चपल - सिद्ध - शुष्क - पक्व - बन्ध, etc.,

will combine to form a सप्तमी - तत्पुरुष. when - meaningfully connected.

Example:

1 अक्षेषु (7th) शौण्डः = अक्षशौण्डः। he is crook in dice

2 अक्षेषु (7th) धूर्तः = अक्षधूर्तः।

3 अक्षेषु कितवः : अक्षकितवः।

4 वीणायां प्रवीणः = वीणाप्रवीणः। skilled in vina.

5 वेदे पण्डितः = वेदपण्डितः। well learned in the veda

6 काव्ये कुशलः = काव्यकुशलः। skilled in the kavyas

7 शास्त्रेषु निपुणः = शास्त्रनिपुणः। Expert in the shastras

8 कार्ये चपलः = कार्यचपलः। restless " " action

9 काश्यां सिद्धः = काशीसिद्धः। acomplished in the kashi.

10 आतपे शुष्कः = आतपशुष्कः। Dried in the sun

11 स्थाल्यां पक्वः = स्थालीपक्वः। cooked in the vessel

12 चक्रे बन्धः = चक्रबन्धः। one who is tied to the wheel.

Here, first 8 examples were विषय सप्तमी and after that 4 Examples were देश - अधिकरण। examples follow.

- A compound 7th case word with the अव्यय - अधि will be explain latter.

Ex: ईश्वरे अधि = ईश्वराधिनः। one who is dependent on ईश्वर

मयि अधि = मदधीनः। one who is dependent on me

त्वयि अधि = त्वदधीनः। = one " " " " you.

2. तीर्थे (7th) ध्वांक्षः इव → तीर्थध्वांक्षः।

तीर्थे (7th) काकः इव → तीर्थकाकः। (ध्वांक्ष = काकः)

This is a type (kind) of a compounding where the compounds indicates निन्दा - censure.

Monday. | 9:15 Am.

Page No. 37

Date 3, 2, 14

so here the तीर्थकाक: refers to a person who is opportunistic (अवसरवादी). or not stay (remaining) in one place. If it is uncompounded it refers to the crow in a तीर्थ-स्थान ।

देवानाम्प्रियः। The word देवानाम्प्रियः is a षष्ठि-तत्पुरुष and an 'अलुक्' समास । here the विभक्ति of the first word पूर्वपद is not dropped. therefore, it is called 'अलुक्' समास । in this example if we make 'अलुक्' समास it conveys 'निन्दा'. and if we make regular समास as देवप्रियः there is not निन्दा ।. (favourite of gods)

ex: कण्ठेकालः। कण्ठे कालः यस्य सः। - बहुव्रीहि

Tuesday. | 9:15 Am.
4/2/14.

Karmadharya TatPurusha = Appositional Determinative

1.2.42 तत्पुरुषः समानाधिकरणः कर्मधारयः । A TatPurusha compound, the case of each member is the same, is called Karmadharya or Appositional Determinative compound. These form a subType of the determinative compounds (TatPurusha). In them the prior part stands as the predicate of the following part, e.g., *black-beetle*, *sky-blue*. The compounds like नीलोत्पलं *blue lotus*, परमात्मा *supreme spirit* etc., are examples of karmadharaya compounds.

There are 8 subTypes of Karmadharya Samasa.

- Visheshana Purvapada Karmadharya, i.e. an Adjective as the prior word
- Visheshana Uttarapada Karmadharya, i.e. an Adjective as the following word
- Visheshana Ubhayapada Karmadharya, i.e. Adjectives as both the first and second words
- Upamana Purvapada Karmadharya, i.e. A Quality or Trait as the prior word
- Upamana Uttarapada Karmadharya, i.e. A Quality or Trait as the following word
- Avadharana Purvapada Karmadharya, i.e. The adverb alone or only governs the meaning
- Sambhavana Purvapada Karmadharya, i.e. A Possibility as the prior word
- Madhyamapada Lopa Karmadharya, i.e. A compound word where an implicit intermediate word is dropped

Tuesday. 9:15 Am
Page No. 33
Date 4 / 2 / 14

* कर्मधारयः = सामानाधिकरण्यम् - तत्पुरुषः।

When 2 words in सामानाधिकरण्यम् combine to form a तत्पुरुषः। And this kind of तत्पुरुषः is called कर्मधारयः।

[1]. विशेषणपूर्वपदः कर्मधारयः।

Examples:

नीलम् उत्पलम् = नीलोत्पलम् । blue lotus.
दीर्घा रज्जुः = दीर्घरज्जुः । Long rope.
उन्नतः वृक्षः = उन्नतवृक्षः।
एकः पुरुषः = एकपुरुषः।
सर्वे देवाः = सर्वदेवाः।
पुराणः पुरुषः = पुराणपुरुषः।
पूर्व पुरुषः = पूर्वपुरुषः।
अपरः पुरुषः = अपरपुरुषः।
प्रथमः पुरुषः = प्रथमपुरुषः।
उत्तमः पुरुषः = उत्तमपुरुषः।
वीरः पुरुषः = वीरपुरुषः।
महान पुरुषः = महापुरुषः। महान् च असौ पुरुषः च।
परमः पुरुषः = परमपुरुषः।

[2] विशेषणोत्तरपदः कर्मधारयः।

Ex: वैयाकरणः खसूचिः = वैयाकरणखसूचिः।

[3]. विशेषणोभयपदः कर्मधारयः।

Ex: कृतम् अकृतम् → कृताकृतम्।
भुक्तम् अभुक्तम् → भुक्ताभुक्तम्।
पितम् अपितम् → पितापितम्।

– These above 3 types of compounds are between words in सामानाधिकरण्यम् । And that सामानाधिकरण्यम् is of the nature of विशेषण - विशेष्य - भाव - सम्बन्धः । that is it belongs to the relationship of adjective and substantive.

This सामानाधिकरण्यम् also exists between an उपमान and उपमेय.

उपमान = example.

उपमेय = exemplified. And कर्मधारय can be formed here also.

[4] उपमानपूर्वपदः कर्मधारयः ।

Here an उपमान (example combines with a quality that is compared to form a कर्मधारयः ।

Example:

1. कुसुमम् इव कोमलम् मनः । (उपमान: कुसुमम्; quality: कोमलम्)

कुसुमकोमलम् = मनः ।

2. वज्रम् इव कठोरम् = वज्रकठोरम् ।

[5] उपमानोत्तरपदः कर्मधारयः । = [उपमेयपूर्वपदः] (metaphor) (रूपक)

Here the उपमेय (exemplified) combines with the उपमान (example) to form a कर्मधारयः ।

Example:

पुरुषः सिंहः इव = पुरुषसिंहः ।

पुरुषः व्याघ्रः इव = पुरुषव्याघ्रः ।

पुरुषः ऋषभः इव = पुरुषर्षभः ।

मुखम् पद्मः इव = मुखपद्मः ।

पुरुषः नागः इव = पुरुषनागः । (नाग = elephant).

हृदय पुण्डरीकं इव = हृदयपुण्डरीकः

Wednesday | 9:15 Am.

Page No. 40

Date 5, 2, 14

6 अवधारणपूर्वपदः कर्मधारयः।

Here, in the विग्रह वाक्य the word, एव is present for emphasis = अवधारणम्। (शब्दों पर जोर देना)

It emphasises the पूर्वपदम्।

Here, also the विशेषण is the 1st word and विशेष्य is the second word.

Example:

विद्या एव धनम् → विद्याधनम्।

गुरुः एव देवः → गुरुदेवः।

तपः एव धनम् → तपोधनम्।

वेदः एव सम्पत् → वेदसम्पत्।

शमादि च तत् षट्कम् कर्म→ शमादिषट्कम् [शमः आदि यस्य सः = शमादि (बहु.)]

शमादि षट्कम् एव सम्पत्तिः कर्म→ शमादिषट्कसम्पत्तिः।

7 सम्भावनापूर्वपदः कर्मधारयः।

Here also a विशेषणम् combines with a विशेष्यम्। However the विशेषणम् is in the form of a name. Here also the पूर्वपद is विशेषणम् and उत्तरपद is विशेष्य.

Example:

अयोध्या इति नगरी = अयोध्यानगरी।

गङ्गा इति नदी = गङ्गानदी।

दशरथः इति राजा = दशरथराजः।

हिमालयः इति पर्वतः = हिमालयपर्वतः।

8 मध्यमपदलोपः समासः कर्मधारयः।

शाक प्रियः यस्य सः =बहु.⇒ शाकप्रियः।

शाकप्रियः पार्थिवः कर्म→ शाकपार्थिवः।

This is a special group of कर्मधारय for which this example is a prototype. Here, already one compound has been formed which has a पूर्वपद.

and a उत्तरपद |. Then, this becomes a विशेषणम् for another विशेष्य | Therefore, a कर्मधारय can be formed, the उत्तरपद of the 1st compound, which now becomes the मध्यमपद of the 2nd compound., is dropped. Still, it is understood.

The 1st compound is a बहुव्रीहि।|

प्रिय: is उत्तरपदम् | शाकप्रिय: is adjective to पार्थिव: | now when कर्मधारय is formed प्रिय is dropped but understood. Therefore, शाकपार्थिव: = The king who likes vegetables.

देवस्य पूजक: $\xrightarrow{GTP}$ देवपूजक: | देवपूजक: ब्राह्मण: $\xrightarrow{\text{कर्म}}$ देवब्राह्मण: |

षोडश संख्याका: पदार्था: ⟶ षोडशपदार्था: |

Where the situation is well known, there alone this compound can take place.

Dvigu TatPurusha = Numeric

2.1.52 संख्यापूर्वो द्विगुः । A compound having a numeral as its prior word is known as Dvigu Samasa.

There are 3 subTypes of Dvigu Compound.

- Taddhitardha Dvigu, i.e. a Dvigu formed using a Taddhita affix
- Uttarapada Dvigu, i.e. a Dvigu having an additional following word
- Samahara Dvigu, i.e. a Dvigu that represents a collection of items

* द्विगुः। A type of तत्पुरुषः

A तत्पुरुष that has a number as the 1st word is called द्विगुः।.

1. तद्धितार्थद्विगुः।

षण्णां मातृणाम् अपत्यम् - The child of six mother.
(षण्णां मातृणाम् → तत्पु. / द्विगु)

षड् + आम् + मातृ + आम्
षड्मातृ + अण् ⟶ षाण्मातुरः।
(अपत्यार्थे तद्धितप्रत्ययः)

Here, the तत्पुरुष between षण्णाम् मातृणाम् is called तद्धितार्थद्विगुः, along with the तद्धित-प्रत्यय (अण्). This प्रत्यय, which has the meaning of अपत्यम् (child), is added and we get षाण्मातुरः।

2. उत्तरपदद्विगुः।

पञ्चगावः धनः यस्य सः ⟶ पञ्चगवधनः।
The one who has 5 cows as wealth

This becomes द्विगु-तत्पुरुष when there is another word (उत्तरपद) to combine to form another Compound. Having a number at begining, it is called द्विगुः।

पञ्च सखायः प्रियः यस्य सः ⟶ पञ्चसखप्रियः।

Here the second Compound will always be a बहुव्रीहिः।

Thursday. 9:15 Am

Page No. 43

Date 6, 2, 14

[3] समाहार द्विगुः ।

When a collection of more than one thing is to be expressed and a number (संख्या) is the 1st word, the compounded word is called द्विगुः ।

The द्विगुः will always be neuter and singular.

पञ्चानाम् गवाम् समाहारः → पञ्चगवम् ।

पञ्चानाम् पात्राणाम् समाहारः → पञ्चपात्रम् । collection of 5 vessels

त्रयाणाम् भुवनानाम् " → त्रिभुवनम् ।

चतुर्णाम् युगानाम् " → चतुर्युगम् ।

सप्तानाम् अह्नाम् " → सप्ताहः m. ।

(exception)

Nan TatPurusha = Anti or Negative

2.2.6 नञ् । The word नञ् *negative,* compounded with another case inflected word results in a Nan TatPurusha compound.

A compound having the word "not" as the prior word is known as Nan Samasa.

There are 5 subTypes of Nan Samasa.

- Nan TatPurusha, i.e. the particle "not" or "no" as the prior word 2.2.6 नञ्
- Ku TatPurusha, i.e. the particle "ku" *meaning reprehensible* as the prior word 2.2.18 कुगतिप्रादयः
- Gati TatPurusha, i.e. particles used in the sense *of having done* as the prior word 1.4.60 गतिश्च , 2.2.18 कुगतिप्रादयः
- Pra-Adi TatPurusha, i.e. one of the 22 prepositions as the prior word 2.2.18 कुगतिप्रादयः
- Upapada TatPurusha, i.e. having a Pratipadika as the prior word 2.2.19 उपपदमतिङ्

* नञ् - तत्पुरुषः ।

[1] A तत्पुरुष समास is formed with negative particle नञ्, as the 1st word being a tatpuruṣa, the compound will be उत्तरपदप्रधान ।.

Example:

न धर्मः = अधर्मः ।	न आत्मा = अनात्मा ।
न सन्देहः = असन्देहः ।	न अश्वः = अनश्वः
न विघ्नः = अविघ्नः ।	न उपलब्धिः = अनुपलब्धिः ।
	न इच्छा = अनिच्छा ।

Rules for नञ् तत्पु. :

In the नञ् - तत्पुरुषः the पूर्वपद is न (न् + अ) when the compounding is done the 'न्' of न is dropped. therefore, न धर्मः = अधर्मः ।

If the second word begins with a vowel the 'अ', which remains after dropping the नकार, gets a न् augment following it. after it comes and becomes 'अन्'. Therefore, we get.

न आत्मा = अनात्मा ।

Note: (Aside) नित्यसमासः ।

Generally when we compound words the पूर्वपद and the उत्तरपदs will be the same in the विग्रहवाक्य and the compound. This kind of विग्रहवाक्य is called स्वपदविग्रहवाक्यः । (its own word)

But in a नित्यसमास either the पूर्वपद or the उत्तरपद will not be present. In place of the absent of पूर्वपद or उत्तरपद another word will be present in the compound The विग्रहवाक्य of this नित्यसमास is called अस्वपदविग्रहवाक्यः ।

In the चतुर्थी तत्पुरुषः ब्राह्मणाय अयम् = ब्राह्मणार्थः । the word अयम् is the उत्तरपद in the वाक्यम् but is absent in the compound. Similarly the word अर्थ is उत्तरपद in the compound but not seen in the वाक्यम्। Therefore, we say the word अर्थ is permanantly in the compound.

चतुर्थ्यन्तं पदम् अर्थेन सह नित्यम् समस्यते।

Here the विग्रहवाक्य is called अस्वपद-विग्रह-वाक्य:। all the नित्यसमासेs will have अस्वपद-विग्रह-वाक्यम्।

* अर्थ used in 4th case meaning is called नित्य।

2. कु समास:

This is also a तत्पुरुष. it is a नित्यसमास।

Here, the अव्यय, कु is the first word of the compound has the meaning of कुत्सित = निन्दित = blameworthy. Here the word 'कु' is नित्यम् (always) as the first word (नित्यम्) where as the (second word) उत्तरपद will keep changing. therefore, it is called a नित्यसमास. Here also the विग्रहवाक्य will be अस्वपदविग्रहवाक्य।.

Examples:

कुत्सित: पुरुष: = कुपुरुष:।

कुत्सिता बुद्धि: = कुबुद्धि:।

कुत्सित: तार्किक: → कुतार्किक:।

3. प्रादि-तत्पुरुष:।

A group of अव्ययs called as प्रादय: = प्र, etc. will combine with a meaningfully connected related word to formed a प्रादितत्पुरुष:। These are also नित्यसमासs and will have अस्वपद-विग्रह-वाक्य:।

प्रादि list = प्रादय:

प्र। परा। अप। सम्। अनु। अव। निस्। निर्। दुस्। दुर्।
वि। आङ्। नि। अधि। अपि। अति। सु। उत्। अभि। प्रति।
परि। उप।

Thursday 9:15 am

Page No. 46

Date 20. 2. 16.

The प्रादि group of अव्ययs can form.

(1) प्रादि तत्पुरुष

(2) प्रादि बहुव्रीहिः

(3) अव्ययीभाव समास

The प्रादि तत्पुरुष is नित्यसमास. Therefore will have अस्वपदविग्रहः।

Example:

शोभनः पुरुषः ⟶ सुपुरुषः।

'शोभन' is substituted by 'सु' ⟶ ∴ नित्यसमास।

शोभनः जनः ⟶ सुजनः।

दुराचारः पुरुषः ⟶ दुष्पुरुषः।

प्र = गतः आचार्यः ⟶ प्राचार्यः। [Past teacher / Retired teacher]

अभि = गतः मुखम् ⟶ अभिमुखम् = "in front of"

प्रति = गतः अक्षम् ⟶ प्रत्यक्षम् [अक्षम् अक्षम् प्रति]

4 उपपद-तत्पुरुष

* उपपदतत्पुरुषः = सोपपदकृत्

This is a kind of 'समास' which comes in the section of तत्पुरुष समास and in the section of कृदन्त. Here the कृदन्त formation and the समास formation are intrinsically (अन्तर्गत) together.

Infact the कृदन्त will form only when a उपपद is present. And the कृदन्त प्रातिपदिकम् which is formed will combine with the उपपद without becoming a पदम् first.

We have seen समास will take place only between two पद's. In that sense this is an exception. The प्रातिपदिक will combine with the उपपद.

उपपद-तत्पुरुष is also नित्यसमासः।

Example: कुम्भं करोति इति → कुम्भम् + (कृ + अण्) denotes the कर्ता

कुम्भम् + (कृ + अण्) (अ) → कुम्भम् + (कार् + अ) → कुम्भ + अम् + कार

कार→प्रातिपदिकम् → कुम्भकार (new समास प्रातिपदिकम्)

→ कुम्भकारः।

→ कुम्भं करोति इति कुम्भकारः।

- भाष्यम् करोति इति → भाष्यकारः।
- सूत्रम् करोति इति → सूत्रकारः।
- चित्रम् करोति इति → चित्रकारः।

* भयम् करोति इति → भयङ्करः।

सोमेन इष्टवान → सोमयाजी। [यज् + णिनि] he did the यज्ञ।

* उष्णम् भुक्तुं शीलम् अस्य - The one who has the nature of eating hot.

उष्णम् + भुज् + णिनि → उष्णभोजिन् (प्रा.) (Like करिन्.) → उष्णभोजी।

* ब्रह्म चरितुम् शीलम् अस्य → ब्रह्मचारी

ब्रह्म + चर् + णिनि → ब्रह्मचारिन् (प्रा.) → ब्रह्मचारिणी (f.) / ब्रह्मचारी (m.)

Nitya Samasa

Some of the compounds discussed are additionally known as Nitya Samasa, i.e. Always Compound. The vigraha vakya or *split into a sentence form* for these compounds is known as *a-sva-pada* vigraha vakya. It means that such a samasa has a word that is *not seen* in its vigraha vakya.

The Nan TatPurusha Samasa subTypes

- Ku TatPurusha Samasa
- PraAdi TatPurusha Samasa
- Upapada TatPurusha Samasa

are also known as Nitya Samasa.

II. Bahuvrihi Samasa = Indeterminate Join Compound

21.2.2014 Fri

Bahuvrihi (name of an ancient acharya)

बहुव्रीहिः समासः

This is a compound in which the compound does not denote either the purva pada or the uttara pada, but denotes a word external to the compound.

> The techincal word उपधा means the penultimate, one but the last

In that sense, it is an adjective to the external word.

eg पीतम् (= yellow) अम्बरं (= cloth) यस्य सः → पीताम्बरः (m 1/1) = कृष्णः (m 1/1) = Lord krishna

Notice, Here the compound does not denote either of the two words of the compound. It refers to Sri krishna, who has a yellow cloth (ie who wears a yellow garment).

Bahuvrihi is of two types.

① समानाधिकरण्य बहुव्रीहिः — this is often found in literature

Here 2 words in same case will combine in an oblique case to denote an external word.

Note: कर्मधारयः compound is all in same 1st case.
Here the 2 words will be in 1st case and will be connected to the external word through any other case, 2nd to 7th.

eg प्राप्तम् (1/1) = उदकम् (1/1) यम् (2/1) = ग्रामम् (2/1) सः । प्राप्तोदकः ग्रामः । {2nd case oblique}
That village to which water has reached.

eg ऊढः (1/1) = रथः (1/1) येन (3/1) = पुरुषेण (3/1) सः । ऊढरथः पुरुषः । {3rd case oblique}
the man by whom the chariot was climbed on.
(ie the man who climbed the chariot)

Note ऊढः (1/1) रथः (1/1) यः (1/1) → will make कर्मधारय compound instead of Bahuvrihi compound.

eg कृतं (1/1) भोजनम् (1/1) येन (m 3/1) सः (1/1) → कृतभोजनः (m 1/1)
आरूढं यानं येन सः → आरूढयानः (m 1/1)
आरूढं यानं यया (f 3/1) सा → आरूढयाना (f 1/1) the girl by whom bus was climbed on

② व्यधिकरण्य बहुव्रीहिः — this is rare

(a) Here the two words will not be in same case and will combine in an oblique case to denote an external word.

(b) The सह bahuvrihi is also an example of this.

Bahuvrihi compound contd. {4th case oblique}

eg दत्ताः[1/1] = पशवः[1/1] यस्मै[4/1] सः → ~~दत्तपशुः~~ दत्तपशुः ।

the one to whom cows were given.

eg पतितानि[1/3] = पर्णानि[1/3] यस्मात्[5/1] सः → पतितपर्णः[1/1] [वृक्षः[1/1] ।] {5th case oblique}

the one from which leaves have fallen. (the autumn trees)

उद्धृतम्[1/1] = ओदनम्[1/1] यस्याः[5/1] सा → उद्धृतौदना[1/1] [स्थाली[1/1] ।]

the one from which cooked rice has been taken out.

eg पीतम्[1/1] अम्बरं[1/1] यस्य[6/1] सः → पीताम्बरः [कृष्णः] । {6th case oblique}

शुक्लम् अम्बरं यस्य सः → शुक्लाम्बरः [ब्रह्मचारी] । dressed in white

निर्मलः[1/1] मनः[1/1] यस्य सः → निर्मलमनाः[1/1]

मनस् declines like नचिकेतस्

eg ~~चि~~ चित्राः गावः यस्य सः → चित्रगुः ।

→ चित्र गो → चित्रगु

eg वीराः पुरुषाः यस्मिन्[7/1] सः → वीरपुरुषः [ग्रामः] । {7th case oblique}

the village of brave men (the village in which brave live)

पठवः छात्राः यस्याम्[7/1] सा → पठुछात्रा [पाठशाला] ।

the school in which students study

2.2.23 शेषो बहुव्रीहिः । All the remaining types of compounds are named Bahuvrihi.

SamadhiKaranya Bahuvrihi

Friday, 9:15 Am.
Page No. 53
Date 21 , 2 , 14.

(3) बहुव्रीहिः।

बहुव्रीहि is a compound, in which the compound does not denote either the पूर्वपद or उत्तरपद (the words of the compound) but denotes a word external to the compound. In that sense it is an adjective to the external word.

Ex: पीतम् अम्बरं यस्य सः ⇒ पीताम्बरः = कृष्णः।

Here the compound does not denote either of the two words of the compound. That is पीतम् (yellow) and अम्बरं (cloth). But it referse to कृष्ण who has (who wears) yellow cloth.

There are two types of बहुव्रीहिः।

(1) सामानाधिकरण्य - बहुव्रीहिः। — This is the common one
(2) व्यधिकरण्य - बहुव्रीहिः। - This is rarer.

1 सामानाधिकरण्य बहुव्रीहिः।

Here two words in सामानाधिकरण्यम् will combine in an oblique case to denote an external word form a बहुव्रीहिः compound. Here the two words which combine will be in first case and will be connected to the external word through any other case (that is 2nd to 7th case).

Examples: 2nd case: प्राप्तम् (1/1) = उदकम् (1/1) यम् (2/1) = ग्रामम् (2/1) सः प्राप्तोदकः (1/1) ग्रामः (1/1)। (यम् → oblique)

The village to reach water has reached.

3rd case: ऊढः (1/1) = रथः (1/1) येन (3/1, → oblique) सः (1/1) → ऊढरथः।
ऊढः (1/1) = रथः (1/1) येन (3/1) = पुरुषेण (3/1) सः → ऊढरथः पुरुषः।

The man by whom the was on.

The man was

" " कृतम् भोजनम् येन सः → कृतभोजनः।
आरूढम् यानं येन सः → आरूढयानः।
आरूढम् यानं यया सा → आरूढयाना। feminine
अधीतः (1/1) वेदः (1/1) येन (6/1) सः → अधीतवेदः। By whom the veda has study.

Camlin Kokuyo

4th case :- दत्तः = पशुः यस्मै सः → दत्तपशुः ।

The one to whom a caw was given

5th case :- पतितानि = पर्णानि यस्मात् सः → पतितपर्णः वृक्षः ।

The trees from whom the leaves was fallen

" " उद्धृतम् = ओदनम् यस्याः सा → उद्धृतौदना स्थाली

The vessel from which the crooked rice was taken out.

6th case :- पीतम् अम्बरम् यस्य सः → पीताम्बरः कृष्णः

शुक्लम् अम्बरम् यस्य सः → शुक्लाम्बरः ब्रह्मचारी one who has white cloth.

7th case :- वीराः = पुरुषाः यस्मिन् सः → वीरपुरुषः ग्रामः ।

पटवः = छात्राः यस्याम् सा → पटुछात्रा पाठशाला ।

चित्राः गावः यस्य सः → चित्रगु → चित्राः गावः = चित्र + गौ → चित्रगु

VyadhiKaran Bahuvrihi

Page No. 55
Date 25/2/14.

2 व्यधिकरण बहुव्रीहिः।

Here two words that are not in सामानाधिकरण्यम् will combine connecting through an oblique case denoting another word to form a this बहुव्रीहि compound. This is an irregular बहुव्रीहिः। therefore rare.

The सामानाधिकरण्यम् बहुव्रीहि is the primary बहुव्रीहिः. We have a freedom to make a सामानाधिकरण्यम् बहुव्रीहि and not a व्यधिकरण बहुव्रीहि। We see the व्यधिकरण बहुव्रीहि in 'शिष्टप्रयोग'. [शिष्ट = learned people of the society]

Example:

गदा ≠ पाणौ यस्य सः → गदापाणिः। (1/1, 7/1, 6/1, 1/1 → 1/1)

भाले ≠ चन्द्रः यस्य सः → भालचन्द्रः। (शिवः / गणेशः) (7/1, 1/1, 6/1, 1/1 → 1/1)
(फालचन्द्रः)

चन्द्रः मौलौ यस्य सः → चन्द्रमौलि। (1/1, 7/1, 6/1, 1/1)

विषम् ≠ कण्ठे यस्य सः → विषकण्ठः। (1/1, 7/1, 1/1, 1/1 → 1/1)

कण्ठे कालः यस्य सः → कण्ठेकालः। (व्यधि. बहु. / 7th अलुक्) (7/1, 1/1 → 1/1)

In this compound कण्ठेकालः the 7th case of the पूर्वपद is not dropped and is retained (व्याकरण सायन्) in the compound. This kind of compound is called अलुक्-समास। Because सप्तमी is not dropped therefore, it is called सप्तमी अलुक् समास.

9:15 Am.

26/2/14. Wednesday

1. सह - बहुव्रीहिः।

A word in 3rd case will combine with the अव्यय 'सह' and form a compound that will denote an external word and form (it is called) a बहुव्रीहि समास.

Note: Here the connecting oblique case of यस्य सः etc., will not be present; Instead the verb 'is' = वर्तते will be present in the विग्रह-वाक्य.

Saha Bahuvrihi

26/2/14. wednesday

1. सह - बहुव्रीहिः।

A word in 3rd case will combine with the अव्यय 'सह' and form a compound that will denote an external word and form (it is called) a बहुव्रीहि समास.

Note: Here the connecting oblique case of यस्य सः etc., will not be present। Instead the verb 'is'=वर्तते will be present in the विग्रह-वाक्य.

wednesday

Page No. 56 Date 26, 02, 14

The अव्यय 'सह' is optionally replaced by 'स'। But Generally only forms with 'स' are seen.

Examples:

पुत्रेण (3/1) सह वर्तते इति → सपुत्रः। सहपुत्रः। The one who is with the son.

कुटुम्बेन (3/1) सह वर्तते इति → सकुटुम्बः। सहकुटुम्बः। The one-who is with the family.

कर्मणा (3/1) सह वर्तते इति → सकर्मकः। (धातुः)

लोम्ना (3/1) सह वर्तते इति → सलोम्नः। (पशुः) लोमन्. = lot of hair

Nan Bahuvrihi

२. नञ् बहुव्रीहिः।

Here the particle नञ् is represented by the प्रातिपदिकम् 'अविद्यमान' in the विग्रहवाक्य। And that नञ् become a first word, combines with another meaningfully related word denoted an external word to form a बहुव्रीहिः।

अविद्यमानः पुत्रः यस्य सः → अपुत्रः one who has no son.

नञ् → न of - नञ् will drop as in नञ् तत्पु.।

Note: The विग्रहवाक्य can also be written as

न विद्यते पुत्रः यस्य सः।

(अस्ति અર્થમાં છે) (બધાં नञ् . तत्पु. માં न drop થાય અને अ જોડાય જાય છે)

अविद्यमानम् अपत्यं यस्य सः → अनपत्यः। No child.

matadi * पृच्छामि - पृच्छ्. ધાતુ ને બે કર્મ હોય છે (1) કોને અને (2) શું પ્રશ્ન પૂછે છે એ રીતે તે દ્વિકર્મક ધાતુઓ છે. આવા કુલ ૨૦ ધાતુઓ છે. જેને બે કર્મ હોય છે

* भू - भवति - I c1, अस् - अस्ति. P. 2c, वृत् - वर्तते - A 1c, विद् - विद्यते A 4c, स्था - तिष्ठति - Ic / सीदति : 1s આ બધા જ Root is अस्ति ના અર્થમાં વપરાય છે

* निपात = અવ્યય - प्रादि = ૨૨ છે. તે બધાં જ અવ્યય છે. પણ જ્યારે તે ધાતુની સાથે આગળ જોડાય છે ત્યારે તે ઉપસર્ગ કહેવાય છે

Pra-Adi Bahuvrihi

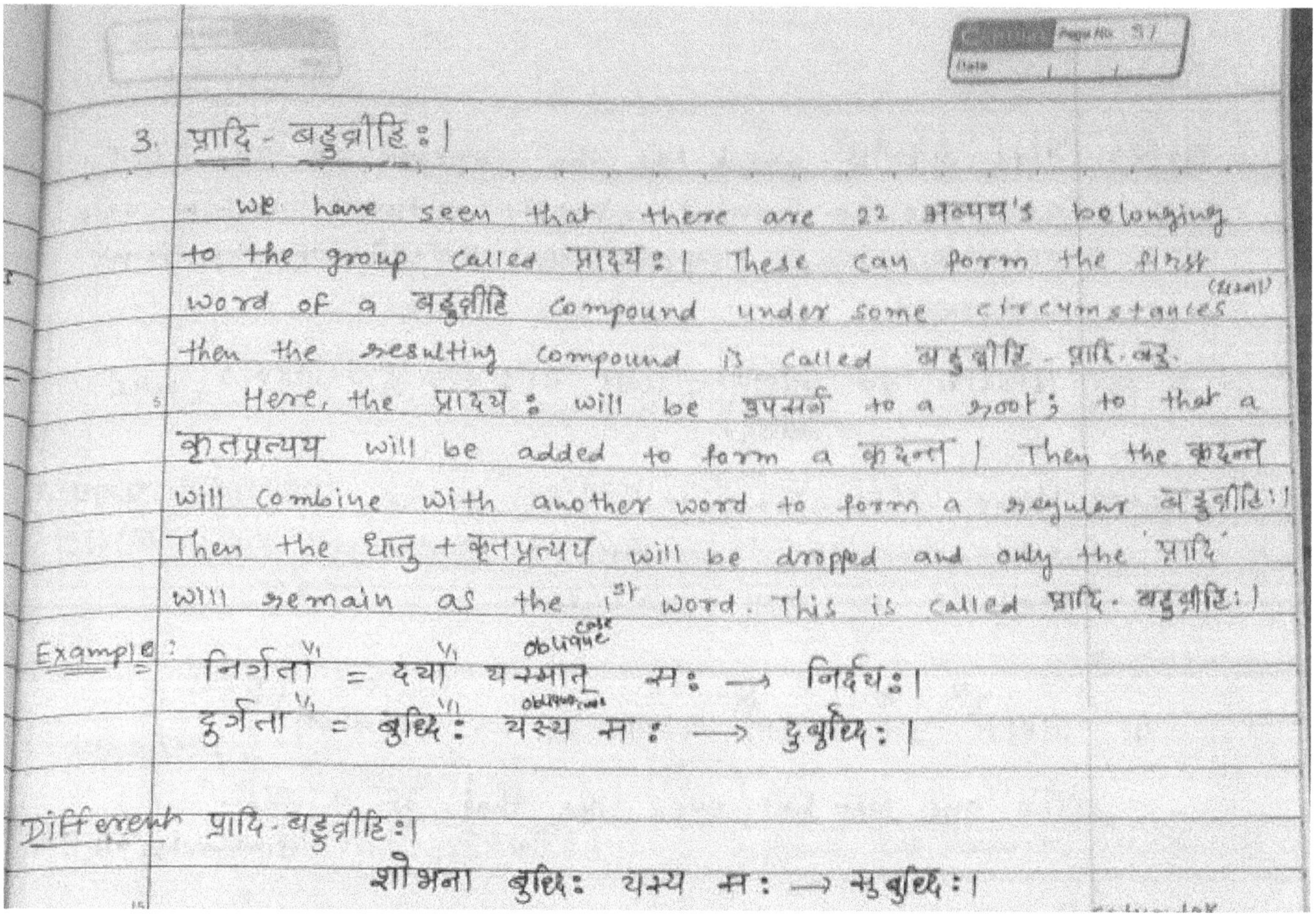

3. प्रादि - बहुव्रीहिः।

We have seen that there are 22 अव्यय's belonging to the group called प्रादयः। These can form the first word of a बहुव्रीहि compound under some circumstances (दशा) then the resulting compound is called बहुव्रीहि - प्रादि-बहु.

Here, the प्रादयः will be उपसर्ग to a root; to that a कृत्प्रत्यय will be added to form a कृदन्त। Then the कृदन्त will combine with another word to form a regular बहुव्रीहिः। Then the धातु + कृत्प्रत्यय will be dropped and only the 'प्रादि' will remain as the 1st word. This is called प्रादि-बहुव्रीहिः।

Example:
निर्गता = दया यस्मात् सः → निर्दयः।
दुर्गता = बुद्धिः यस्य सः → दुर्बुद्धिः।

Different प्रादि-बहुव्रीहिः।
शोभना बुद्धिः यस्य सः → सुबुद्धिः।

Madhyamapada Lopi Bahuvrihi

Saturday 1/03/14 9:15 am

4. मध्यमपदलोपी (उत्तरपदलोपी) बहुव्रीहिः।
उपमान पूर्वपद बहुव्रीहिः। (Both are same)

Here there is a comparison (सादृश्यम्) involved and in the context (पूर्वापर संबंध विवक्षा) उपमान the बहुव्रीहि is formed. Here generally there is a first compound which will be a तत्पुरुष and another compound is formed dropping the second word of the first compound.

Example:

1. गजस्य आननम् —6TP→ गजाननम्
गजाननम् इव आननम् यस्य सः → गज + आनन + आनन
→ गजानन् प्रा. → गजाननः ¹/₁ ।

The one who has (got) face like that of an elephant.

2. उष्ट्रस्य मुखम् इव मुखं यस्य सः → उष्ट्रमुखः।

Date

Note: This बहुव्रीहि which has the context of an उपमान can also be formed directly without making two steps and then dropping the उत्तरपद of the first compound.

3. Eg: पुण्डरीके इव अक्षिणी यस्य सः → पुण्डरीकाक्षः। Lotus अक्षिन्.

Note: Here this compound has some समासान्त प्रत्यय added to it. Therefore, it becomes पुण्डरीकाक्षः। details we will see later.

4. जलजे इव अक्षिणी यस्याः सा → जलजाक्षी f¹/₁ जलज = fish

The one who has eyes like that of a fish.

Similarly, मीनाक्षी

DikAntaraLakshana Bahuvrihi

5. दिगन्तरालक्षणः बहुव्रीहिः। *Only this much [illegible] in Dak: 9/3/14 [illegible] 19/1/15*

The directions northeast, northwest, Southeast and Southwest are called as दिगन्तराः दिशाः। The word denoting these directions are बहुव्रीहिः।

* दक्षिणस्याः च पूर्वस्याः च दिशः यदन्तरालम् = दक्षिणपूर्वा = आग्नेयी दिक् (Southeast)

* पूर्वस्याः च उत्तरस्याः च दिशः यदन्तरालम् = पूर्वोत्तरा = ईशानी दिक् (Northeast)

* उत्तरायाः च पश्चिमायाः च दिशः यदन्तरालम् = उत्तरपश्चिमा = वायवी दिक् (Northwest)

* पश्चिमायाः च दक्षिणस्याः च दिशः यदन्तरालम् = पश्चिमदक्षिणा = नैर्ऋती दिक् (west south)

III. Dvandva Samasa = Equal Force Join Compound

2.2.29 चार्थे द्वन्द्वः । When a set of several case affixed words stand in a relation expressable by च *"and"*, then the set so compounded is called Dvandva Compound.

Itaretara Dvandva

Saturday. Page No. 59 Date 01 . 03 . 14. 9:15 Am

* द्वन्द्व समासः ।

We saw that तत्पु-समास was उत्तरपदप्रधानः । and अव्ययीभावः was पूर्वपदप्रधानः । and बहुव्रीहिः was अन्यपदप्रधानः । In all these what we mean by the word "प्रधान" is that the compound represents / denotes that word.

In contrast in a द्वन्द्व all the words gain equal representation. That is all the words are denoted therefore, द्वन्द्वः is called सर्वपदप्रधानः ।

(1) इतरेतर द्वन्द्वः । (2) समाहार द्वन्द्वः ।

1. इतरेतर द्वन्द्वः ।

Example:

रामः च लक्ष्मणः च गच्छतः । } meaning are same
रामलक्ष्मणौ गच्छतः । } Rāma and Laxmana are going.

Here two nouns connected to one क्रियापद are combined to form one word. Even in the compound, both words are independently connected to the verb. Both are denoted by the verb. therefore, the verb is in dual this is called इतरेतर-द्वन्द्वः ।

Example:

हरिः च हरः च → हरिहरौ ।
ईश्वरः च कृष्णः → ईश्वरकृष्णौ ।
शिवः च केशवः → शिवकेशवौ ।
ग्रीष्मः च वसन्तः च → ग्रीष्मवसन्तौ ।
इन्द्रः च अग्निः च → इन्द्राग्नी ।
माता च पिता च → मातापितरौ ।

Samahara Dvandva

2. समाहार द्वन्द्वः।

We have seen while defining a समास that समास itself has a sense of unification but here in the द्वन्द्व there is an additional (sense of) unification. All the elements (घटकाः) of the द्वन्द्व are unified into one entity. such a द्वन्द्व is added समाहार द्वन्द्वः।

As a result of unification the Gender also will become neuter. So the समाहार द्वन्द्व will always be neuter and singular.

Ex: घटः च पटः च → घटपटम्।

घटश्च पटश्च अनयोः समाहारः → घटपटम्।

Here the speaker has the freedom either to do the unification (समाहार) are not.

But there are some well known द्वन्द्व समास's in the language which are always unified they are called as नित्यसमाहारद्वन्द्व's. (नित्यत्वम् for समाहारद्वन्द्वः)

Example:

पाणी ($f^{1/2}$) च पादौ ($m^{1/2}$) च एतेषां समाहारः → पाणिपादम् ($n^{1/1}$)।

insects like bees: यूकाः ($m^{1/3}$) च लिक्षाः ($f^{1/3}$) च एतेषां समाहारः → यूकालिक्षम् ($n^{1/1}$)।

This is a compound which is always unified (नित्यसमाहारः) because it is a compound of द्वन्द्व of क्षुद्र (small) animals.

Que: From where does the smallness of animals begin?

Ans: "Beginning with नकुल → आनकुलात् जन्तवः क्षुद्राः"।

अहिः च नकुलः च अनयोः / एतेषां (unification of the two) समाहारः → अहिनकुलम्।

Here the reason for समाहार is that there is permanent enemity between them.

IV. AvyayiBhava Samasa = Adverbial Compound

2.1.5 अव्ययीभावः । Adverbial Compounds. These are Indeclinable.

Avyaya Purvapada AvyayiBhava

Monday. | 9:15 Am.
Page No. 61
Date 03, 03, 14

* अव्ययीभावः ।

अव्ययीभावः is a compound in which the पूर्वपद in an अव्यय । After compounding the compound itself becomes an अव्यय therefore, it will not decline in all विभक्ति's and numbers barring exceptions it will take neuter 1st case always.

- Generally most of the अव्ययीभाव's are नित्यसमास and will have अस्वपदविग्रहवाक्य ।
- The अव्यय's will combine only in (सोमपाद वायु) particular meanings.
- They can be divided (विभाजित) into 3. categoryes.

(1) अव्ययपूर्वपदः in which the अव्यय is पूर्वपद । (first word).
(2) अव्ययोत्तरपदः in which the अव्यय is उत्तरपद । (second word)
(3) अव्ययपदरहितः in which there is No अव्यय than also it is अव्ययीभाव compound

[1] अव्ययपूर्वपदः अव्ययीभाव समास ।

1. विभक्त्यर्थ — हरौ → अधिहरि । (અહીં) અધિ ઉપસર્ગ લાગે છે જે માત્ર અધિકરણના અર્થમાં જ વપરાય છે).
— हरौ वार्ता प्रवर्तते ।
— अधि हरि वार्ता प्रवर्तते । (प्रत्यय added and dropped also.)

हरौ → हरि + ङि (7/1) → हरि + अधि (↑ represents 7th case) → (by some rule अधि will come first प्रा.) अधिहरि → (अव्यय) अधिहरि + सु (n 1/1) (पदम्) → अधिहरि ⇒ with reference to हरि.

- अधिभूतम् = with reference to भूत's (elements)
- अधिदैवम् = w.r.t दैव's (देवता's)
- अध्यात्मम् = w.r.t आत्मा

2. समीपार्थ – कृष्णस्य समीपम् → उपकृष्णम् (near कृष्ण)

the वाक्यम् is कृष्णस्य समीपम्। Now to form the compound in the sense of 'समीप' we will use the अव्यय 'उप' and form the अव्ययीभाव-compound.

कृष्णस्य समीपम् → कृष्णस्य उप → कृष्ण + ङस् + उप
→ उपकृष्ण (प्रा.) → उपकृष्णम् (ए1 पदम्)।

3. समृद्ध्यर्थ –

In the sense of prosperity (समृद्धि) the अव्यय 'सु' is used.

मद्राणां समृद्धिः → मद्राणां सु → मद्र + आम् (6/3) + सु
→ सुमद्र (प्रा.) → सुमद्रम् (ए1 पदम्)

The prosperity of the मद्र-देश

ऋद्धि = prosperity → समृद्धिः → great prosperity
विगता ऋद्धिः → व्यृद्धिः → Decline of prosperity

4. व्यृद्ध्यर्थ – In the sense of 'Decline of prosperity' the अव्यय 'दुर्' is used.

यवनानां व्यृद्धिः → दुर्यवनम् Decline of the prosperity of the यवनs (रोमन, ग्रीक आदि)

5. अर्थाभावार्थ – अर्थ here has the meaning of 'some substance' (धन, वस्तु, तात्पर्य). In the sense of absence (अभाव) of 'something', the अव्यय 'निर्' is used to form a अव्ययीभाव compound.

मक्षिकाणाम् अभावः → निर्मक्षिकम्।

6. अत्ययार्थे – अत्यय = destruction (नाश). (અહીં અવ્યય/અવ્યય અતિ નો અર્થ નાશ થાય)

हिमस्य अत्ययः → अतिहिमम् ।

7. असम्प्रत्यर्थे – "not proper now"

सम्प्रति = now, (હમણાં), असम्प्रति = not now, but here "Not proper now" (ઉચિત અર્થ).

निद्रा सम्प्रति न युज्यते → अतिनिद्रम् ।

8. शब्दप्रादुर्भावे – In the sense of presenting a subject, 'इति' is used.

हरिशब्दस्य प्रकाशः → इतिहरि । इत्युपनिषद् - has been presented.

9. पश्चादर्थे – पश्चाद् = later, following something – in that sense 'अनु' is used.

विष्णोः पश्चात् → अनुविष्णु = After विष्णु / following viṣṇu

10. with यथा ।

'यथा' has four meanings and compound can be made in all meanings, but different अव्यय's are used in the compound.

(1). योग्यतार्थे – fitness → in this sense 'अनु' is used. "in keeping with".

रूपस्य योग्यम् = अनुरूपम् = in keeping with the form

(2). वीप्सा – व्याप्तुम् इच्छा – The desire to cover every object = Actually it means "each & every".

अर्थं अर्थं प्रति = प्रत्यर्थम् = with reference to each and every object.

(दिने दिने → प्रतिदिनम्). - meaning is same but not under this compound.

③ पदार्थ - अनतिनिवृत्यर्थ = In the sense of "not transgressing". (આયદાનું ઉલ્લંઘન)

शक्तिम् अनतिक्रम्य = यथाशक्ति । not transgressing ones capacity or In keeping with one's capacity.

- यथामति = मतिम् अनतिक्रम्य
यथाबुद्धि = बुद्धिम् अनतिक्रम्य
यथेच्छम् = इच्छम् अनतिक्रम्य

④ सादृश्यार्थ →

हरेः सादृश्यम् → सहरिः = Similar to हरिः।

5/03/16
Wednesday
9:15 Am.

Note: The अव्यय 'यथा' has the meaning of सादृश्यम् and in place of यथा सह is used, and replacement for सह is स ।

11. आनुपूर्व्यार्थे ।

आनुपूर्व्यम् = क्रमः । (એક પછી એક / one after one-ther)

one after another / in the order of arrangement

To say ज्येष्ठस्य आनुपूर्व्येण = "following the elder in the order of happening."

the Compound will be अनुज्येष्ठम् । In the sense of आनुपूर्व्यम्, अनु is used.

- अनुज्येष्ठम् दाशरथयः रामः, भरतः, लक्ष्मणः च शत्रुघ्नः भवन्ति।

In the descending order from eldest to youngest the sons of Daśarath are Rāma, Bharata, Lakṣmana and Śatrughna.

- अनुकनिष्ठम् दाशरथयः शत्रुघ्नः, लक्ष्मणः, भरतः च रामः भवन्ति।

In the descending order from youngest to the eldest of Daśaratha are Śatrughna, Lakṣmana, Bharata and Rāma.

Contd.

12. यौगपद्यार्थे । युगपत् = 'together', 'at once'.
यौगपद्यम् = togetherness.

In the sense of togetherness the अव्यय 'सह' is used to form an अव्ययीभाव compound. And when 'सह' is used as the first word of a compound it is replaced by 'स'.

चक्रेण युगपत् = सचक्रम् । together with the चक्रम् (discus) ।

हरिः सचक्रम् शंखं धारयति । Hari sports (wears) the conch (शंख) along with the discus (चक्र).

13. सादृश्यार्थे । In the sense of 'similar' 'सह' is used to form an अव्ययीभाव compound. And 'सह' is replaced by 'स' ।

सख्या सदृशः - ससखि । - one who is like his friend.

14. सम्पत्त्यर्थे - Here 'सह' is used in the sense of wealth and combines with another word to form an अव्ययीभाव compound.

क्षत्राणां सम्पत्तिः - The wealth of the क्षत्रियs → सक्षत्रम्

15. साकल्यार्थे । = साकल्यम = complete without anything remaining. सकलस्य भावः । = साकल्यम

कलया सह वर्तते इति सकलः । तस्य भावः सकलम् । बहु.

तृणमपि अपरित्यज्य अत्ति । = He eats everything along with grass also. सतृणम् अत्ति ।

16. अन्तार्थे । अन्तः = end., In the sense of 'up to the end' or 'up to' 'सह' is used; सह is replaced by 'स' ।
(usually we use पर्यन्त in this sense).

अग्निग्रन्थपर्यन्तम् अधीते = साग्नि अधीते । (क्रियाविशेषण અવ્યયીભાવ)

(જે વેદ વિદ્યાર્થી ભણે છે તે અગ્નિગ્રંથ સુધી ભણેલો છે.)

17. अवधारणार्थे = यावत् is (the अव्यय) used.

यावत् = as many as there are.

Here in the compound, it is used in the sense of "as many as there are, only so many are present"

यावन्ति नामानि यावन्नाम । As many names as there are, so many.

यावदुक्तम् । यावद्दत्तम् ।

18. मर्यादार्थे → The अव्यय आङ् (आ) is used to indicate मर्यादा = exclusive limit.

आ हिमालयात् → आहिमालयम्
(तेन विना) up to the Himalayas excluding Himalayas

मर्यादा
- मर्यादा — Exclusive limit — तेन विना
- अभिविधि: — inclusive limit — तेन सह

19. अभिविध्यर्थे :-

आ हिमालयात् → आ हिमालयम् | up to the Himalayas including the Himalayas.

Both same we can say → आहिमालयम् तेन सह

20. आभिमुख्यार्थे = आभिमुख्यम् = 'facing something', 'towards'.

In this sense the अव्यय 'प्रति' is used.

अग्निं प्रति → प्रत्यग्नि उपविशति ।

Avyaya Uttarapada AvyayiBhava

2. अव्ययोत्तरपदः अव्ययीभावः समासः ।

मात्रार्थे = मात्रा = measure. In the sense of some measure the अव्यय 'प्रति' is combined with any सुबन्तम् पदम् to form an अव्ययीभाव compound. Here the 'प्रति' becomes the 2nd word and has the meaning of 'little'.

शाकस्य लेशः — शाकप्रति । सूपप्रति ।

Avyaya Padarahita AvyayiBhava

3. अव्ययपदरहितः अव्ययीभावः समासः ।

1. तिष्ठद्गु प्रभृतीनि ।

These are some compounds which look like बहुव्रीहि but are अव्ययीभाव compounds same in the language as such. Therefore, pāṇini simply places them as they are in this group of अव्ययीभाव compounds. That is he does 'निपातम्'.

तिष्ठन्ति गावः यस्मिन् काले दोहनाय → तिष्ठद्गु कालम् । (दोहनकालम्)

The time when cows stand

आयत्यः गावः यस्मिन् काले → आयतीगवम् कालम् ।

The time when the cows come home.

सम्प्रति = now

असम्प्रति = not now.

विषमम् =

प्रदक्षिणम् = walking around.

अप्रदक्षिणम् =

Friday. 7/3/14 9:15 Am.

2. पारेशब्दयुक्तः । गङ्गायाः पारे → पारेगङ्गम् - Across the गङ्गा

3. मध्येशब्दयुक्तः । समुद्रस्य मध्ये → मध्येसमुद्रम् ।
महाभारतस्य मध्ये → मध्ये-महाभारतम् ।

Both 'पारे' & 'मध्ये' are 7th case words. The 7th case has been drop in compound formation and later an 'ए' is added as a 'निपातम्'.

B. Keval Samasa = Simple Word Join Compounds

These compound words are simply joins of two case inflected words. 2.1.4 सह सुपा ।

* केवलसमासः ।

तत्पुरुषादिसंज्ञाविनिर्मुक्तः समाससंज्ञामात्रयुक्तः केवलसमासः

पूर्वं भूतः → भूतपूर्वः ।

पूर्वं अभूतः → अभूतपूर्वः ।

उत्तमः ऋणे → उत्तमर्णः । The one who gives a loan

अधमः ऋणे → अधमर्णः ।

वागर्थौ इव → वागर्थाविव (रघुवंश)

आजन्म शुद्धानाम् → आजन्मशुद्धानाम् one who is pure from birth

अवश्यं स्तुत्यः → अवश्यस्तुत्यः surely to be praise.

Some Other ways of looking at Samasa

Some other word constructions may also *said to be compounded*.
एकशेषः । We can see Eksesha as an exception to Dvandva Samasa. e.g.
माता च पिता च → पितरौ , भ्राता च स्वसा च → भ्रातरौ , हंसः च हंसी च → हंसौ , सः च सुनिलः च → तौ ।

अ-लुक्-समासः । When Case affix of prior word is not dropped. e.g.
आत्मनेपदम् → This is actually a 4th case TatPurusha compound.
युधिष्ठिरः → This is actually a 7th case TatPurusha compound.

नित्य-समासः । Always Compounded. e.g. ब्राह्मणाय अयम् → ब्राह्मणार्थः । *this is for the Brahmin.*

असमर्थ-समासः । Incomplete Compound. e.g. असूर्यम्पश्याः । *the sun cannot be seen.*

21.Jan.2014 Tue
पञ्चमी कृष्ण पौष

Lesson 64.
समास-विचार:
Samas Vichar.

A long long time ago, everything that needed to be passed from generation to generation was done in the form of verse. Verse was the only means of ensuring that knowledge was protected. It may have been years since we've left school, but who has forgotten 'Jack and Jill'? Prose, on the other hand, has been relegated to the back alleys of our mind.

In the midst of all this poetic creativity, a natural problem reared its head. Sanskrit is the only language in the classical world which makes use of प्रत्ययs. The use of प्रत्यय s helps every single word to have an identity and a meaning of its very own. But fitting the word + प्रत्यय into a metre in verse form was a difficult task indeed. "What to do?" asked a poet. "No problem! Let's create a shortcut," said another. And समास came into being. समास, स म स was the original SMS... Short Message Service. Be proud guys, we created it!!!!!!

I kid you not. There does exist such a verb: अहं समस्यामि does indeed mean 'I am creating a synopsis.... or in our layman terms... a shortcut.'
समास allows a person to string two words together to form one single word. And "ishortcut ishtyle" the first word is written without an appropriate प्रत्यय. For example instead of saying राज्ञ: पुत्र: I'd say राजपुत्र: and still make complete sense.
Why does Devdas have to romance his love with a long drawn out, "You have such a beautiful face just like the moon!" All he'd do is say "अयि चन्द्रमुखि" Devdas too, by the way, is a समास word. देवस्य दास: , देवदास: । The difference between a सन्धि: and a समास: would be that in the former, two letters combine to form a single whole letter or a conjoined letter(either in the middle of a word or between two words to form a single word) and in the

1

27/49
Month 17

compare how a verb denotes. Rama goes → Verb denotes agent here. Forest is gone to by Rama → Verb denotes object here. Rama is going → Bhave, Verb denotes itself here, Inner abstract meaning.

पूर्वपदप्रधान: 1. अव्ययीभाव: A word which conveys a meaning, is a part of the समास which, after the combination of the two words, becomes an अव्यय।
For example: Here the 1st word is an Avyaya, indeclinable. Case n/1
add सु to indicate सौभाग्य 'lots of goodness.' सुमङ्गलम् = मङ्गलानां समृद्धिः lots of auspiciousness.

Here, the 1st word is denoted and takes precedence.

उत्तरपदप्रधान: 2. तत्पुरुषः In this समास, the second word of the समास is given importance. For example: देवदासः = देवस्य दासः। The first part of the word is simply an apt description of the second. We are talking about the दासः here and not the देवः। TP Samasa takes all cases. Case of final word.

Here, the 2nd or last word is denoted & takes precedence.

Adjective + Substantive eg. दशरथपुत्रः

3. कर्मधारयः In this समास, one word is an adjective of the other. It is a part of the तत्पुरुषः, but we shall list it separately for convenience's sake. For example: नीलोत्पलम् = नीलम् उत्पलम्। A 1TP is also called कर्मधारय. (प्रथमा विभक्ति TP) = सामानाधिकरणम्

→ In same case, gender, no

(the 8th type of तत्पुरुषः)

(the 9th type of तत्पुरुषः)

4. द्विगुः In this समास, which is a part of the कर्मधारयः, the first word is a number; how many in a collection of things. For example : पञ्चवटी = पञ्चानां वटानां समाहारः।

सर्वपदप्रधान: 5. द्वन्द्वः Be sure to look out for the च between words in the विग्रहः of this समासः!!! For example: हरिहरगुरवः/हरिगुरुहराः =हरिश्च हरश्च गुरुश्च। Only samasa with more than 3 words.

Substantive + Substantive

All words are equally important and denoted.

अन्यपदप्रधान: 6. बहुव्रीहिः When two words are put together to imply something totally different, बहुव्रीहिः is what you see. For example: चन्द्रमौलिः = चन्द्रः मौलौ यस्य सः। Here, we are neither giving importance to the moon or to the forehead but the Person who is adorned so: Shiva.

A Bahuvrihi is an Adjective

The compound denotes a word external to it.

7. अलुक्समासः is not really a different समासः। Whenever, two words are put together and the विभक्ति of the first word remains intact,

Broadly there are 4 types :- 1. अव्ययीभाव 2. तत्पुरुष 3. बहुव्रीहि 4. द्वन्द्व
In Avyayibhave and in Tatpurusha, only two words can combine at a time. Whereas; in Bahuvrihi and Dvandva, more than two words can combine at a time. However, it is rare to see more than 3 words forming a Bahuvrihi. On the other hand, n-number of words are seen in the literature combining to form a Dvandva.

29/49
Month 17

समासः द्विविधः → केवलसमास
→ विशेषसमासः – 1., 2., 3., 4.

22.1.2014 Wed

1. समसन समासः Putting two or more words together into one word is called समासः

eg समसन (वन) eg दशरथस्य पुत्रः → दशरथपुत्रः

सीतायाः पतिः → सीतापतिः

2. समासः सुबन्तानाम् पदानाम् भवति, न तु तिङन्तानाम् पदानाम् ।

Q. How to know it is Samasa. A लौकिक, then समासः takes place. Depending on the समासः itself, it can be any of the above समासः s. For example: युधिष्ठिरः = युधि स्थिरः ।

8. नञ्समासः is not really a different समासः । Whenever you wish to convey 'the absence' of something, this समासः is used. For example: अविघ्नः = न विघ्नः । A type of तत्पुरुषः ।

10th again a type of तत्पुरुषः 9. उपपदसमासः see how the noun is described here.. अभयङ्करः = अभयं करोति इति । It is formed by pratipadika + हलादि असर्वनामस्थान Vibhakti

समासः is a vast topic. Sorry, I made a mistake, a **VAST TOPIC**. We need to be practical about such things. We can't handle it all at this stage. Let's go over a few details to help us decode what we may most often come across. A tabular column will help.

1. अव्ययीभावसमासः । 3.3.2014

You will recognize the अव्ययीभावसमासः in words

1. Where the first part of the word is an अव्यय or a निपात (निपाताः are particles which possess no gender, and number and the case termination after which is dropped or elided. For example चादयः (च and others) and प्रादयः (प्र and others).
2. The second part of the word is a noun (सञ्ज्ञा).
3. The combined word is an अव्यय and is नपुं. एकवचनम् ।
4. The combined word समस्तपदम् is different from the विग्रहः, because the conveys a अव्यय special meaning to the noun.

Addition of अव्यय to mean		समस्तपदम्	विग्रहः
अधि	in, on	अधिहरि	हरौ इति

3. समासः युगपत् द्वयोः द्वयोः सुबन्तयोः भवति ।

द्वन्द्वे तु बहूनाम् अपि ।

eg राज्ञः पुरुषः → राजपुरुषः → राजपुरुषस्य आगमनम् → राजपुरुषागमनम्

In case of द्वन्द्व, eg रामः[1/1] च कृष्णः[1/1] च हरिः[1/1] च —द्वन्द्व→ रामकृष्णहरयः[1/3]

eg रामः च शत्रुघ्नः च द्वन्द्व रामशत्रुघ्नौ[1/3] ie बहूनाम् सुबन्तानाम् पदानाम् युगपत् समासः भवति।

उप closeness	उपकृष्णम्	कृष्णस्य समीपम्
निस् or निर् absence	निर्जनम्	जनानाम् अभावः
अनु behind/ following	अनुरथम्	रथस्य पश्चात्
प्रति every	प्रतिदिनम्	दिनं दिनम्
यथा in that manner	यथाशक्ति no spelling error here. There is no visarga. All these words are अव्ययs remember?	शक्तिमनतिक्रम्य
स with/ resembling	सजनकम्	जनकेन सह /जनकस्य सादृश्यम्
आ beyond / upto	आहिमालयम् आमुक्ति आबालवृद्धम्	आ हिमालयात् (चीनदेशः) आ मुक्तेः (मुक्ति तक, मुक्ति के पूर्व) a life span (!!)
बहिः outside	बहिर्ग्रामम्	ग्रामात् बहिः
अनु near/ towards	अनुकूलम्	towards the bank
प्रति a) away from (opposite of the meaning in the above row) b) repetition	प्रतिकूलम् प्रतिदिनम्	against the bank दिने दिने
सु abundance, prosperity	सुमद्रम्	मद्राणां समृद्धिः
दुर् adversity, poverty	दुर्यवनम्	यवनानां व्यृद्धिः

5

4. परस्परान्वितयोः[6/2] सुबन्तयोः[6/2] एव[φ] समासः[1/1] भवति[III/1]।
mutually connected — only — become

ie two mutually connected subantam padams alone will become a compound. The mutual connection should be a meaningful connection, as in example below

eg भवति[III/1] दर्शनम्[1/1] राज्ञः[6/1] पुरुषः[1/1] अमात्यस्य[6/1] धावति[III/1]। 31/49 Month/7

eg पश्य भार्या[1/1] राज्ञः[6/1] पुरुषः[1/1] देवदत्तस्य[6/1] स्तः।
look wife of king, man of Devdutta standing.

अति destruction, end of	अतिहिमम्	हिमस्य अत्ययः
अति inappropriate	अतिनिद्रम्	निद्रा सम्प्रति न युज्यते
इति utterance of sound	इति हरि	हरिशब्दस्य प्रकाशः
आ a) starting from b) uptil	a) आजन्म b) आमरणम्	a) जन्मनः आरभ्य b) मरणपर्यन्तम्

2. तत्पुरुषसमासः ।

तत्पुरुषसमासः is that समासः wherein the first word-part's विभक्ति-प्रत्यय is dropped. Depending on which विभक्ति-प्रत्यय that first part would have taken if broken into it's विग्रहः, the तत्पुरुषसमासः is given that particular name. For example: द्वितीयातत्पुरुषः ।

Go over the short explanation of तत्पुरुषसमासः at the very beginning of this lesson.

> Note: The word तत्पुरुषः itself will help you remember what समासः this involves. तस्य पुरुषः = तत्पुरुषः !!

A sammasa can be made only between two words that are meaningfully connected through a karaka. In these two examples, the राज्ञः (6/1) and पुरुषः (1/1), are not connected meaningfully so for these words compounding cannot (should not) be done.

23.1.14 Thu

5. समासे पूर्वं श्रूयमाणं पदं पूर्वपदम् । उत्तरत्र श्रूयमाणं पदम् उत्तरपदम् ।

What is heard first in a smasa is called puurvapadam. What is heard next is called uttarapadam.

eg चोरात् (5/1) भयम् → चोरभयम्

There are definite rules to which word will be placed first. Those we will see later.

3 कूपे पतितः → कूपपतितः one fallen in the well

4 ग्रामं गतः → ग्रामगतः one gone to the village

5 मार्गात् अत्यस्तः → मार्गात्यस्तः one given up the path (veered away)

[The samastpadam will decline like रामः] संशयम् आपन्नः → संशयापन्नः one with a doubt

		समस्तपदम्	विग्रहः
द्वितीयातत्पुरुषः	4	शरणागतः	शरणम् आगतः
Here, the पूर्वपदम् can	2	दुःखातीतः	दुःखम् अतीतः one who has crossed over sorrow.
be any word.	1	कृष्णश्रितः 1/1	कृष्णं 2/1 आश्रितः 1/1 one who is dependent on krishna alone
	6	ग्रामप्राप्तः one who has reached the village	ग्रामं प्राप्तः
However, the उत्तरपदम्	3	शोकपतितः	शोकं पतितः one drowned in sorrow
can be only one of ten	5	मेघात्यस्तः	मेघम् अत्यस्तः
given words.	7	भयमापन्नः one filled with fear	भयम् आपन्नः
	8	ग्रामगमी one who goes to village	ग्रामं गमी [one who has the nature of always going to the village.
	10	अन्नबुभुक्षुः one desirous of eating food	अन्नं बुभुक्षुः 9 → ग्रामंगामी]

6. The process of compounding :-
- → meaning full connection of karaka seen
- → application of grammatical rules Vibhakti/Sandhi
- → 2 subantam padams from a sentence are taken

eg दशरथस्य 6/1 पुत्रः 1/1 रामः 1/1 वनं 2/1 गतवान् 1/1 PAP ।

→ दशरथस्य (padam) पुत्रः (padam) —6TP→ दशरथ (pratipadika) + ङस् (6/1) + पुत्र (pratipadika) + सु (1/1) —drop case affix and do sandhi→ दशरथपुत्र (intermediate pratipadika) + सु (1/1) → दशरथपुत्रः (Samasa समस्तम् पदम्)

लौकिक-विग्रह-वाक्यम् अलौकिक-विग्रह-वाक्यम्

→ दशरथपुत्रः 1/1 रामः 1/1 वनं 2/1 गतवान् m1/1 ।

eg दशरथस्य 6/1 पुत्रेण 3/1 रावणः 1/1 हतः m1/1 PPP ।

we take out the 2 subantam padams with meaningful connection and compound them and then place the compound back in the sentence.

दशरथपुत्रेण 3/1 रावणः 1/1 हतः 1/1 । Ravana was killed by Dashrath's son.

eg दशरथस्य 6/1 पुत्रं 2/1 हनुमान् 1/1 पश्यति III/1 ।

→ दशरथपुत्रं 2/1 हनुमान् 1/1 पश्यति III/1 । Hanumana sees Dashrath's son.

33/49

Month 17

3TP :- Here also the 2nd word is fixed. Rule1: A word in 3rd case meaningfully connected to one of the following words only, combines to form तृतीया तत्पुरुष ।
The उत्तरपद s here are पूर्व, सदृश, सम, ऊनार्थ, कलह, निपुण, मिश्र, संमिश्र, श्लक्ष्ण, and अवर । Here, ऊनार्थ is a collection of words having meaning 'less', 'little less'.
Rule2: संस्कारद्रव्य (3/1) + अन्नवाचिशब्द (1/1) will form → तृतीया पुरुष समास: (that which improves the quality forms a samasa)

eg संस्कारद्रव्य = दधि, अन्नवाचि = ओदन → दध्योदन:, क्षीरोदन:

28.1.14 तृतीयातत्पुरुष:	बाणाहत: hit by arrow	बाणेन आहत:
दधि } ओदन } दध्योदन:, क्षीरोदन:	खड्गहत: killed by spear	खड्गेन हत: passive present participle
	शिवात्रात:	शिवया त्रात:
	शिवत्रात:	शिवेन त्रात: protected by shiva
ऊन = विकल = हीन = less → ऊनार्थ शब्दौ	विद्याहीन:	विद्यया हीन: ④
ie hard crunchy eatable	ज्ञानशून्य:	ज्ञानेन शून्य: ④
(someone) who is like a mother	मातृसदृश:	मात्रा सदृश: ②
	पितृतुल्य:	पित्रा तुल्य: ④
protected by Hari	हरित्रात:	हरिणा त्रात:
	तत्कृतम्	तेन कृतम्
	कालिदासरचितम्	कालिदासेन रचितम् composed by kalidas
prior by a month	मासपूर्व:	मासेन (3/1) पूर्व: (1/1) ①
like a father	भ्रातृसम:	भ्रात्रा सम: ③
कार्षापणेन ऊनम् → कार्षापणोनम् = less by a quarter coin	धान्योनम् less by a whisker	धान्येन ऊनम् ④ less by a grain.
कार्षापणेन विकलम् → कार्षापणविकलम् = less by a quarter coin	धान्यविकलम्	धान्येन विकलम् ④
	वाक्कलह:	वाचा कलह: ⑤
आचारेण (3/1) निपुण: (1/1) → आचारनिपुण: (1/1)	आचारकुशल:	आचारेण कुशल: ⑥
mixed with shakkar	शर्करामिश्रम्	शर्करया मिश्रम् ⑦
endowed with sweetness	गुडयुक्तम्	गुडेन युक्तम् ⑦
आचारेण श्लक्ष्ण: → आचारश्लक्ष्ण: by good conduct, due to good conduct	कुट्टनश्लक्ष्णम्	कुट्टनेन श्लक्ष्णम् ⑨
less by a month	मासावर:	मासेन अवर: ⑩

eg मिश्रीकरणम् with a भक्षम्
गुडेन (m 1/3) पृथुका: (poha) → गुडपृथुका:
गुडेन (m 1/3) धाना: (grains) → गुडधाना:

nice, pleasing ie कर्तरि तृतीया or करणे तृतीया

Rule3: Any word in 3rd case denoting कर्ता or करणम्, will combine with a meaningful related कृदन्तपदम् (=verb) and form 3TP. Many such compounds.

eg शिवेन त्रात:
eg कालिदासरचितम्
eg परशुविच्छिन्नम्
eg खड्गहत:
eg खड्गछिन्न:

***And that is the sole reason why you cannot have दण्डताडितवान् as a तृतीया तत्पुरुष: । ताडितवान् is a Present active participle and doesn't fit with the rules stated above. Instead, you may have a दण्डताडित: । Gottit?**

→ present passive participle

Fri 24.1.2014

A तत्पुरुष: समास: is of 4 types

a) सामान्य: which is further of 7 types because of 7 vibhaktis for a word. 8

b) कर्मधारय: which is further of 8 types

c) द्विगु: which is further of 3 types

d) नञ्-प्रभृतय:

बहुलम् = exceptions, extensions; usage → by a saint, by a great person

Note: In this rule there is no restriction on the पूर्व or पर words.

There is a word 'बहुलम्' in this sutra, because of that, some unintended words are also included in this 3TP. Again, some words that could have been compounded, are not (should not) compounded. eg * eg. नृपः ग्रामस्य अर्धं आचार्याय ददाति । Vigraha vakya

→ नृपः (1/1) अर्धग्रामम् (1TP 2/1) आचार्याय (4/1) ददाति (III/1) । compounded sentence

eg. पूर्वम् (n 1/1) कायस्य (m 6/1) → पूर्वकायः (m 1/1) , अपरम् (n 1/1) भवनस्य (n 6/1) → अपरभवनम् (n 1/1)

	समस्तपदम्	विग्रहः
29.1.14 चतुर्थीतत्पुरुषः	कुण्डलहिरण्यम्	कुण्डलाय हिरण्यम्
Limited Scope of words.	यूपदारु	यूपाय दारु
only specific way of	कुम्भमृत्तिका	कुम्भाय मृत्तिका
combination.	द्विजार्थः for eg: सूपः	द्विजाय अयम्
	छात्रार्था for eg: यवागूः	छात्राय इयम्
	शिश्वर्थम् for eg: दुग्धम्	शिशवे इदम्
	भूतबलिः for offering to living beings	भूतेभ्यो बलिः
	गोहितम् for the sake of cows	गवे हितम्

Note:
The compound गुरुदक्षिणा cannot be separated into गुरवे दक्षिण । The विग्रहः has to be गुरोः दक्षिणा ।

A special type of कर्मधारय तत्पुरुष compound is defined here.

The प्रथमा-तत्पुरुषः (1TP) कर्मधारय :- अवनय अवयव

(i) When there is a relationship of a 'part' to the 'whole' there the word denoting the 'part' joins with the word denoting the 'whole'.

→ Words denoting the part can only be one of पूर्व = before, front, first
अपर = upper, above
अधर = below, lower
उत्तर = later, second, last, above, and upper
अर्ध (n) = half

→ Words denoting the whole can be anything.

eg अर्धं (n 1/1) ग्रामस्य (m 6/1) —1TP→ अर्ध + सुँ + ग्राम + ङस्
पूर्वपद उत्तरपद
drop intermediate affixes → अर्धग्राम

परवत्लिङ्गं अर्धग्रामः (m 1/1)
give the gender of the पर word ie the second word
{ Note, the case will depend on how this compound fits in the actual sentence!

Only a neuter अर्ध, but other पूर्व etc in any gender.

Note: In any द्वन्द्व or तत्पुरुष compound the gender of the compound is the same as that of the last word therein.

35/49
Month 17

Note: The samasa denotes the last word.

ie उत्तरपदप्रधानः तत्पुरुषः eg अधरं (n 1/1) गृहस्य (n 6/1) → अधरगृहम् (n 1/1)

PRONOUNCIATION NOTE: for ह्न and ह्म only:
pronounce the hn as nh [aspirated n]
pronounce the hm as mh [aspirated m]

सर्पात् भीः → सर्पभीः fear from snake

Limited in scope, Limited in formation	समस्तपदम्	विग्रहः
30/1/14 पञ्चमीतत्पुरुषः	चोरभयम् fear from thief	चोरात् भयम्
Rule 1. Any word in 5th case will	वृकभीतिः fear from	वृकात् भीतिः
combine only with भय-भीत-भीति-भी	व्याघ्रभीतः one who is afraid from tiger	व्याघ्रात् भीतः
इत्येतैः शब्दैः and form a STP.	अयशोभीः fear from	अयशसः भीः
Panini, this rule is restricted (a)	ग्रामनिर्गतः one who has come away from village	ग्रामात् निर्गतः
four words as 2nd words in the compound. (b)	अधर्मजुगुप्सुः one who refrains from adharma	अधर्माद् जुगुप्सुः
	स्वर्गपतितः fallen from heaven	स्वर्गात् पतितः
	पापमुक्तः one who has been freed from sin	पापात् मुक्तः
Exceptions	अन्तिकादागतः	अन्तिकात् आगतः (अन्तिक)
	दूरादागतः	दूरात् आगतः (दूर)
	स्तोकान्मुक्तः	स्तोकात् मुक्तः (स्तोक)

According to Panini, this rule is restricted to the above four words as 2nd words in the compound.
You cannot form STP with any other words
eg चोरात् रक्षितः → चोररक्षितः CANNOT be made.
But in the usage, some other examples are seen by Bhashyakara. They are (a), (b)

Rule 2: Some words in 5th case will combine with अपेत-अपोढ-मुक्त-पतित-अपत्रस्त शब्दैः to form STP.
eg सुखात् अपेतः → सुखापेतः one who has moved away from happiness.
कल्पनायाः अपोढः — one who has moved away from imagination
Note:

Note: Exception: There is a rule that the word रात्रि (f) will become रात्र (m) masculine if it is at the end of the समासः।

eg उत्तर (n 1/1) रात्रेः (f 6/1) → उत्तररात्रः (m 1/1)

Extension to Exception: The following रूढि words are there that do not follow the above. Shivaratri, Navratri, Shubhratri

(ii) All the words denoting part एकदेश wrt time, will combine with a word denoting time.

eg. अहन् (m) = day   अह्नः (6/1)   { Note it is अहन् and not अह्न! and अहन् = अह्न

मध्यम् (1/1) अह्नः (6/1) —1TP→ मध्य + सु (1/1) + अहन् + ङस् (6/1) —drop affix→ मध्यअह्न —sandhi→ मध्याह्न —gender conversion→ मध्याह्नः (m 1/1) (noon time)

पूर्वम् (1/1) अह्नः (6/1) —1TP→ पूर्वाह्नः —णत्वम् sandhi→ पूर्वाह्णः (m 1/1) morning

अपरम् (1/1) अह्नः (6/1) —1TP→ अपराह्नः —णत्वम्→ अपराह्णः (1/1) afternoon

मध्यम् (1/1) रात्रेः (6/1) —1TP→ मध्यरात्रः (m 1/1) midnight

सायम् (φ) अह्नः (6/1) —1TP→ सायाह्नः (1/1) evening

27.1.2014 Only a fixed few words will be used to form the द्वितीयातत्पुरुषः

Rule: Any word in 2nd case will combine with only one of श्रित, अतीत, पतित, गत, अत्यस्त, प्राप्त, आपन्न, गामी, गमि, गामी and बुभुक्षु when they are meaningfully connected.

Note: Therefore we cannot make a compound of अन्नं बुभुक्षवान्.

31.1.2014 The most common compound is 6TP in the usage.

	समस्तपदम्	विग्रहः
षष्ठीतत्पुरुषः	राजपुरुषः man of the king	राज्ञः (6/1) पुरुषः (1/1) king's man
Rule: Any word in 6th case will combine with any meaningfully related word to form a 6TP.	देवपूजकः	देवस्य पूजकः
	ईश्वरभक्तः	ईश्वरस्य भक्तः
	देवालयः	देवस्य आलयः
	सर्वमहान्	सर्वेषां महत्तरः
	सर्वश्वेतः	सर्वेषां श्वेततरः
Exceptions	-	अन्नस्य पाचकः (अक प्रत्ययः)
Let us derive मदाचार्यः मम आचार्यः →(6TP) अस्मत् + ङस् + आचार्य + सुँ		धनस्य हर्ता (तृच् प्रत्ययः)
अस्मत् replaced by मत् in singular → मत् आचार्य →(जश् sandhi) मदाचार्यः	-	जगतः स्रष्टा (तृच् प्रत्ययः)
Also see derivation of plural		घटस्य कर्ता (तृच् प्रत्ययः)
कल्पनापाठः: अस्माकं (6/3) आचार्यः (1/1) →(6TP) अस्मत् + ङस् + आचार्य + सुँ →(sandhi) अस्मदाचार्यः		ब्राह्मणस्य कर्तव्यम् (तव्य प्रत्ययः)
eg तरङ्गात् अपत्रस्तः → तरङ्गापत्रस्तः one who has been thrown from the waves	-	ब्राह्मणस्य कृत्वा (अव्यय)
		राज्ञां पूजितः (क्त प्रत्ययः added to पूज्)

दशरथस्य (6/1) पुत्रः (1/1), विद्यायाः आलयः, मम (6/1) आचार्यः (1/1) my teacher

7TP examples: ईश्वरे (7/1) अधि → ईश्वराधीनः dependent on God; मयि (7/1) अधि → मदधीनः dependent on Me

In 5TP, the पर पदम्s are all fixed as mentioned. In addition, scope of पूर्व पदम्s are also limited. How to know? Look for usage by elders. eg प्रासादात् पतितः will not combine. It looks like पतितः has more meaning than simple physical falling.

	समस्तपदम्	विग्रहः
सप्तमीतत्पुरुषः	वीणाप्रवीणः skilled in the Veena	वीणायां प्रवीणः
	वेदपण्डितः learned in Veda	वेदे पण्डितः
	काव्यकुशलः expert in poetry	काव्ये कुशलः
7TP Rule: A word in 7th case will combine with धूर्त - शौण्ड - कितव - प्रवीण - पण्डित - कुशल - निपुण - चपल - सिद्ध - शुष्क - पक्व - बन्ध, etc, to form a 7TP when meaningfully connected.	शास्त्रनिपुणः clever in scriptures	शास्त्रेषु निपुणः
	कार्यचपलः restless in action	कार्ये चपलः
	जललीनः	जले लीनः
	जलमग्नः	जले मग्नः
eg अक्षेषु शौण्डः →(7TP) अक्षशौण्डः (cheater in dice - shakuni)	कार्यचतुरः	कार्ये चतुरः
	स्थालीपक्वः cooked in vessel	स्थाल्यां पक्वः

The पर पदम्s have a meaning of 'crook' or 'clever'.

चक्रे बन्धः → चक्रबन्धः tied to wheel

आतपे शुष्कः → आतपशुष्कः dried in the sun

Note: 7TP with the avyaya अधि will be explained later.

Note:- The examples given here are विषय सप्तमी (adjective/subject matter). Also look at words that are देश सप्तमी. eg 11

A finer understanding of grammar using an example of 3TP

वाचा (3/1) कलहः (1/1) → वाच् + टा (3/1) + कलह + सुँ (1/1) → वाच् + कलह →(चोः कुः कुत्वम् Sandhi) वाक्कलहः

→ The pratipadikam here is वाच्

→ when for compounding we drop the प्रत्ययs, the resulting words got are treated as padas (and not pratipadikams) for the sake of applying sandhi rules etc. Hence the वाच् becomes वाक् by application of कुत्वम् sandhi which applies on पदान्त only.

37/49
Month 17

	समस्तपदम्	विग्रहः
प्रादि तत्पुरुष	प्राचार्यः	प्रगतः आचार्यः
	प्रपितामहः	प्रगतः पितामहः
	अतिमर्यादः	अतिक्रान्तः मर्यादम्
	प्रत्यक्षः	प्रतिगतः अक्षम्
	उद्वेलः	उद्गतः वेलाम्
	निर्गृहः	निर्गतः गृहात्

Basant Panchami
4.2.2014 Tue

इत = **3. कर्मधारयसमासः ।** सामानाधिकरण्य - तत्पुरुषः ।

Two words in सामानाधिकरण्यम् combine to form a तत्पुरुषः । And this kind of तत्पुरुषः is called कर्मधारयः

This one is really simple. Whenever two words, one which is an adjective of the other, are combined, you have a कर्मधारयसमासः । So you will have a combination of a विशेषण and a विशेष्य, an उपमान and an उपमेय । Since one is a विशेषण of the other, naturally, when a विग्रहः is formed, both the words will be in the same विभक्तिः। Adjective + Substantive

You may see the words च असौ, इव, एव, in the विग्रहः to reinforce the relationship between the two words.
सु meaning "beautiful/ good" and कु (कुत्सित) meaning "bad" are added to words to form a कर्मधारयसमासः। eg दशरथः इति राजा → दशरथराजः । महान् : इति राजा → महाराजः

Q Why pratipadika राजन् was not used here?

Note : A Some extra प्रत्ययs come into play for some samasa That we are not doing

> **Note:**
> **Why has this particular समासः been called कर्मधारयः? Simple.**
> **Let's look at an example... नीलोत्पलम् । उत्पलं नीलवर्णं धारयति । नीलं becomes the object in the sentence.**
> **Similarly, गुरुदेवः । गुरुः देवस्य पदं धारयति । Alternatively it could be: देवः गुरोः रूपं धारयति । If you look at the examples in the tabular column, you'll begin to see how one of the words "becomes" the object of the other.**
> **Even if that may not be an authentic explanation, why must we reject it if it helps us remember what the कर्मधारयसमासः is?!!**

29.1.14 4TP:- Rule 1 The तादर्थ्ये चतुर्थी will combine to form a 4TP when there is a प्रकृति - विकृति (cause-effect) भाव सम्बन्ध between two words.
eg. कुण्डलाय (4/1) हिरण्यम् (1/1) → कुण्डलहिरण्यम् (1/1), यूपाय (4/1) दारु (1/1) → यूपदारुम् (1/1)
Here the हिरण्यम् (gold) (effulgent) and दारु (wood) are प्रकृतिs (causal) → 4th case meant for the कुण्डल (earring) and यूप (sacrificial post, flagstaff) are विकृतिs (products) → for the sake of, and there is तादर्थ्ये चतुर्थी connection between them. Hence compounding occurs.

Rule 1: विशेषणपूर्वपदः कर्मधारयः (first word is adjective)

Rule 2: विशेषणउत्तरपदः कर्मधारयः (second word is adjective)

Rule 3: विशेषणोभयपदः कर्मधारयः (both are adjectives)

These compounds are between words in सामानाधिकरण्यम्, and this is in the form of विशेषण - विशेष्य - भाव - सम्बन्धः ie. it belongs to the relationship of adj. & subs.

Rule 4: उपमानपूर्वपदः कर्मधारयः

Rule 5: उपमानोत्तरपदः कर्मधारयः

Rule 6: अवधारणपूर्वपदः कर्मधारयः
Here in the vigraha vakya the word एव is present for emphasis ie अवधारणम् of पूर्वपदम्. eg △

Rule 7 सम्भावनापूर्वपदः eg∞

कर्मधारयसमासः	समस्तपदम्	विग्रहः
Such combinations are very common in	महादेवः	महान् च असौ देवः
english language! Ha!	कृष्णसर्पः	कृष्णः सर्पः
	नीलोत्पलम् blue lily	नीलम् उत्पलम्
पुराणः पुरुषः → पुराणपुरुषः	दीर्घरज्जुः long rope	दीर्घा रज्जुः
उत्तमः पुरुषः → उत्तमपुरुषः	* कुसुमकोमलम् as soft as a flower (example + quality)	कुसुमम् इव कोमलम् मनः (exemplified)
	चन्द्रमुखम्	चन्द्र इव मुखम्
उन्नतः वृक्षः → उन्नतवृक्षः tall tree	※ मुखपद्मम्	मुखं पद्मम् इव
एकः पुरुषः → एकपुरुषः one man	※ मुखकमलम्	मुखं कमलम् इव
सर्वे देवाः → सर्वदेवाः	※ पुरुषसिंहः	पुरुषः सिंहः इव
कृतम् अकृतम् → कृताकृतम् done-not done	कृष्णश्वेतः	कृष्णश्च श्वेतश्च (both are adjectives)
	स्नातानुलिप्तः	स्नातश्च अनुलिप्तश्च (क्त प्रत्ययान्त विशेषणs)
भुक्तम् अभुक्तम् → भुक्ताभुक्तम्	चराचरम्	चरश्च अचरश्च (opposites)
	गुरुदेवः	गुरुः एव देवः
वज्रम् इव कठोरम् मनः	△ विद्याधनम्	विद्या एव धनम्
→ वज्रकठोरम् मनः	△ तपोधनम्	तपः एव धनम्
a mind that is hard as a diamond	△ वेदसम्पत् (compare tattvabodha शमादि षट्क सम्पत्ति)	वेदः एव सम्पत्
	∞ अयोध्यानगरी	अयोध्या इति नगरी
पुरुषः ऋषभः → पुरुषर्षभः	आम्रवृक्षः	आम्रः इति वृक्षः
पुरुषः नागः → पुरुषनागः snake like man alert	कुपुत्रः	कुत्सितः पुत्रः
चन्द्रः वदनम् → चन्द्रवदनम्	कुमाता	कुत्सिता माता
शमः आदि यस्य सः → शमादिः	सुपुरुषः	शोभनः पुरुषः
शमादिः च तत् षट्कम् कर्मधारय → शमादिषट्कम्	सुजनः	शोभनः जनः
शमादिषट्कम् एव सम्पत्तिः कर्मधारय → शमादिषट्कसम्पत्तिः	स्वागतम्	शोभनम् आगतम्

This सामानाधिकरण्यम् can also exists between an उपमान and उपमेय. (ie example and exemplified).

कर्मधारयः can be formed here also. eg * Here an उपमान combines with a quality that is compared to form a कर्मधारयः

Again, उपमेय can combine with उपमान. eg ※ ie metaphor.

cause, offering, happiness, protection, words with such meaning

4TP Rule 2 The तादर्थ्ये चतुर्थी will combine with हित, बलि, सुख and रक्षित when they are meaningfully connected to form a चतुर्थी-तत्पुरुषः।

13

eg भूतेभ्यः (4/3) बलिः (1/1) → (भूतबलिः) (1/1) (offering for living beings)

गवे (4/1) सुखम् (1/1) → (गोसुखम्) (1/1) (for happiness for the cow))

○ = pratipadikam ie the पूर्वपदम् is in pratipadikam form.

गवे (4/1) रक्षितम् (1/1) → गोरक्षितम् (1/1) (protection for the cow))

39/49 Month 17

Rule 7 contd ∞
Here also the पूर्वपदः is विशेषणम् and उत्तर पदः is विशेष्यम्. But the विशेषणम् is in the form of a name. अयोध्या इति नगरी → अयोध्यानगरी
गंगा इति नदी → गङ्गानदी, हिमालय इति पर्वतः → हिमालयपर्वतः

5.2.14 Rule 8 मध्यमपदलोपः कर्मधारयः eg शाकः प्रियः यस्य सः —Bahu vrihi→ शाकप्रियः पार्थिवः

This is a special group of कर्मधारयः for which this eg is a prototype. Here already one compound has been formed which has a पूर्व and उत्तर पदs. Then this compound itself becomes an adjective for another substantive and therefore कर्मधारयः can be formed.

When such a कर्मधारयः is formed, the उत्तरपदः of the 1st compound (ie मध्यमपदः of 2nd compound) is dropped. Still it's presence is understood intuitively.

The 1st compound is a Bahuvrihi. Here, शाकपार्थिवः means the king who likes vegetables.

Note: This compound can take place only where a situation is well known. रूढ़ event.

4. द्विगुसमासः ।

(संख्या) समास with numbers!! Just the examples themselves will help you figure out what is what! A no. as the पूर्वपदः is called द्विगुः । Derivation is complex!

Rule① तद्धितार्थ द्विगुः eg षड् + आम् + मातृ + आम् → षड्मातृ + अण् (anubandhika)

द्विगुसमासः	समस्तपदम्	विग्रहः
In षाण्मातुरः the	पञ्चगवम् (a collection of 5 cows)	पञ्चानां गवां समाहारः षण्मातृ + अण् (because of अपत्यम्)
तद्धित प्रत्ययः अण्	पञ्चपात्रम् (the 5 puja vessels)	पञ्चानां पात्राणां समाहारः
has the meaning of child	त्रिभुवनम्	त्रयाणां भुवनानां समाहारः
Note: तद्धित means	चतुर्युगम् /चतुर्युगी	चतुर्णां युगानां समाहारः → षाण्मातुरः
because of	सप्ताहः	सप्तानाम् अह्नां समाहारः
	नवरात्रम् / नवरात्री	नवानां रात्रीणां समाहारः
Rule② उत्तरपदः द्विगुः eg A. Here पञ्च गावः will become a द्विगुः because there is a following word ie उत्तरपदः	त्रिलोकी	त्रयाणां लोकानां समाहारः (अकारान्त – लोक – केवलं स्त्रीलिङ्गे)
that is धनम् here; and a number in the beginning. eg पञ्च सखायः प्रियः यस्य सः → पञ्चसखप्रियः	पञ्चमूली	पञ्चानां मूलानां समाहारः (अकारान्त – मूल – केवलं स्त्रीलिङ्गे)
one who has 5 friends dear to him. Note: Here the second compound will always be bahuvrihi	पञ्चवटी	पञ्चानां वटानां समाहारः (अकारान्त – वट – केवलं स्त्रीलिङ्गे)
6.2.14 Rule③ समाहारद्विगुः	शताब्दी	शतानाम् अब्दानां समाहारः
When a collection of more than one thing is	षाण्मातुरः (child of 6 mothers)	षण्णां मातॄणाम् अपत्यम्
to be expressed and a no. is the first word. eg ∞	द्वैमातुरः	द्वयोः मात्रोः अपत्यम्
This samasa will always be	A पञ्चगवधनः (the one who has 5 cows as wealth)	पञ्च गावः धनं यस्य सः
nominative singular neuter. Exception – सप्ताहः	पञ्चखट्वी / पञ्चखट्वम्	पञ्चानां खट्वानां समाहारः (आकारान्त – खट्वा)

Note: We are learning compounds to be able to understand vedas and not to start composing compounds!

4TP Rule3 The तादर्थ्ये चतुर्थी will combine with the word अर्थ as 14a नित्यसमास ( ) and form 4TP. Here the word अर्थ itself has the meaning of प्रयोजनम् (for the sake of). Even though this is a तत्पुरुषः, it is an adjective to an external word (ie not to the पर word). And this kind of तत्पुरुषः can be used in all the three genders.

eg ब्राह्मणाय (4/1) अयम् (1/1) सूपः (1/1) → ब्राह्मणार्थः सूपः

छात्राय (4/1) इयम् (1/1) यवागू → छात्रार्थी यवागू

कर्म धारय: शाकपार्थिव: । eg. देवस्य पूजक: → देवपूजक: | eg षोडशसंख्याका: पदार्था:
देवपूजक: ब्राह्मण: कर्म → देवब्राह्मण: । कर्म → षोडशपदार्था: ।
Srinivasan is Pujya Swamiji's secretary. He is fondly called Coffee Srinivasa ie Coffee liking Srinivasa.

5. द्वन्द्वसमास: । 1.3.2014

Just take a look at the examples. Easy.

Between every word, be sure to add the च . A compound of two words will be dual and a compound of more than two will be in the plural in the spelling of the dvandva. A point to be noted is that words beginning with a vowel and words ending in अकारान्त should come first.

समस्तपदम्	विग्रह:
हरिहरौ	हरिश्च हरश्च (इकारान्त words before अकारान्त)
ईशकृष्णौ	ईशश्च कृष्णश्च (two boys named Ishvara and Krishna resp.)
अश्वरथेन्द्रा: / इन्द्राश्वरथा:	अश्वश्च रथश्च इन्द्रश्च
शिवकेशवौ	शिवश्च केशवश्च
ग्रीष्मवसन्तौ	ग्रीष्मश्च वसन्तश्च
हेमन्तशिशिरवसन्ता:	हेमन्तश्च शिशिरश्च वसन्तश्च
मातापितरौ	माता च पिता च
पाणिपादम्	पाणी च पादौ च एतेषां समाहार:
रथिकाश्वारोहम्	रथिकाश्च अश्वारोहाश्च एतेषां समाहार:
काकोलूकम्	काकश्च उलूकश्च अनयो: समाहार:
पुत्रपौत्रम्	पुत्रश्च पौत्रश्च अनयो: समाहार:
दासीदासम्	दासी च दासश्च अनयो: समाहार:
पुत्रपौत्रम्	पुत्रश्च पौत्रश्च अनयो: समाहार:

एकाशेष: a part of the द्वन्द्वसमास: ।

Note: Here the sentence where the compounding takes place is :-
ब्राह्मणाय अयम् सूप: । the compounding is taking place between ब्राह्मणाय and अयम् । But the अयम् is not included in the compound. The second word brought in is अर्थ that has the meaning of 'purpose'.

eg. बालाय इदं पय: → बालार्थं पय: । Milk for the boy
→ बालाय अर्थ: → बाल + ङे + अर्थ + सु → बालार्थ → (Sandhi)
विशेष्य लिङ्ग: बालार्थं पय: ।
particular gender comes in

Wed 26.2.2014 (b) सह बहुव्रीहिः A word in 3rd case will combine with the avyaya सह and form a compound that denotes an external word. Here the connecting oblique case of यस्य सः etc, will not be present. Instead the verb = is = वर्तते will be present in the Vigraha vakya. The avyaya सह is optionally replaced by स । ~~But~~ Generally forms with स are seen.

When similar things are put together and the entire compound is described by just one of the words, either in the dual or plural, एकाशेषः is seen.

समस्तपदम्	विग्रहः
वृक्षौ	वृक्षश्च वृक्षश्च
पितरौ	माता च पिता च
भ्रातरौ	भ्राता च स्वसा च
पुत्रौ	पुत्रश्च दुहिता च
हंसौ	हंसश्च हंसी च
तौ	स च रामश्च
यौ	स च यश्च
भवन्तः	भवन्तश्च भवत्यश्च
वयम्	यूयं च वयं च
रामौ	रामश्च रामश्च

यस्य सः **6. बहुव्रीहिः** 21.2.2014 Fri.

Read our simple explanation again of this particular समासः (given at the beginning of the lesson) then let's move on. You'll find either both the words of the विग्रहः in the same विभक्तिः or they may be in different विभक्तिःs.

Since we are talking about someone else altogether, you need to describe the compound by adding a यं सः, येन सः, यस्याः सा and the like.

In other cases you'll see compounds formed by a combination of सह with the तृतीया विभक्तिः।

4TP contd

Because it is permanently compounded in this manner, it[16] is called नित्य समासः. Further, as we see in the examples, this समासः is an adjective to an external word.

30.1.14 These 4TP compounds ending in Artha (अर्थ) can be used as Kriya विशेषणम् Adverb. Such use is very common. eg भोजनार्थम् (2/1) भोजनशालां (2/1) गच्छति (III/1) for the sake of eating he goes to dining hall.

eg पठनार्थम् (2/1) पाठशालां (2/1) गच्छति (III/1) । for the sake of studying he goes to school.

eg पुत्रेण सह वर्तते इति → सपुत्रः [सहपुत्रः] one who is with a son.

कुटुम्बेन सह वर्तते इति → सकुटुम्बः one who is with family.

कर्मणा सह वर्तते इति → सकर्मकः धातुः

लोम्ना सह वर्तते इति → सलोमनः पशुः one who is hairy

Note:

The word बहुव्रीहि: itself means "a person who has plenty of rice". In other words, a wealthy man. A long time ago, parents would give their daughter in marriage to Mr. बहुव्रीहि:, who would have the capacity to look after their child well. It won't be difficult now to connect this word to what the समास: implies.

	समस्तपदम्	विग्रह:
same विभक्ति:		
	प्राप्तोदक:	प्राप्तम् उदकं यं स:
	हतशत्रु: (राजा)	हता: शत्रव: येन स:
	कृतभोजन:	कृतं भोजनं येन स:
	अधीतकाव्या	अधीतं काव्यं यया सा
	धृतपुष्पा	धृतानि पुष्पाणि यया सा
	दत्तभोजनम् (भिक्षुक:)	दत्तं भोजनं यस्मै स:
	उद्धतौदना (स्थाली)	उद्धत: ओदन: यस्या: सा
	पतितपर्ण: (वृक्ष:)	पतितानि पर्णानि यस्मात् स:
	गलितपुष्पा (लता)	गलितानि पुष्पाणि यस्या: सा
	रूपवद्भार्य:	रूपवती भार्या यस्य स:
	गङ्गाभार्य:	गङ्गा भार्या यस्य स:
	दृढाभक्ति:	दृढा भक्ति: यस्य स:
	similarly : पीताम्बर:, दशानन:, चतुरानन:, चतुर्मुख:, पद्मयोनि:	
	वीरपुरुष: (ग्राम:)	वीरा: पुरुषा: यस्मिन् स:
Different		

17

31-1-14 GTP Contd. see derivation of 'Your' युष्मद्

तव पादम् → (GTP) युष्मत् + ङस् + पाद + सुँ → (युष्मत् replaced by त्वत् because it is singular) त्वत् + पाद → (जश् sandhi) त्वद् पाद → (चर् sandhi) त्वत् पादम् → त्वत्पादम्

Your foot

eg Plural 6/3 युष्माकं पुस्तकानि → (GTP) युष्मत्पुस्तकानि

43/49 [illegible]
Month 17

26.2.2014 contd (c) नञ् बहुव्रीहि Here the particle नञ् is represented by the pratipadika अविद्यमान in the vigraha vakya. That नञ् becomes the first word, combines with another meaningfully related word, to denote an external word.

विभक्तिःs.		
	गदापाणिः	गदा पाणौ यस्य सः
	गडुकण्ठः	गडुः कण्ठे यस्य सः
	भालचन्द्रः	भाले चन्द्रः यस्य सः
	चन्द्रमौलिः	चन्द्रः मौलौ यस्य सः
	विषकण्ठः	विषं कण्ठे यस्य सः
	कण्ठेकालः	कण्ठे कालः यस्य सः
with सह	सपुत्रः / सहपुत्रः	पुत्रेण सह वर्तते इति (पुत्रेण सहितः)
	सकुटुम्बः / सहकुटुम्बः	कुटुम्बेन सह वर्तते इति
	सकर्मकः	कर्मणा सह वर्तते इति
	सलोमकः	लोम्ना सह वर्तते इति
	महायशस्कः / महायशाः	महत् यशः यस्य सः (कप् is added because no other rule is applied to यशस् when forming the compound)
	उदात्तमनस्कः / उदात्तमनाः	उदात्तं मनः यस्य सः (कप् is added because no other rule is applied to मनस् when forming the compound)
कप् is also added when the last word is a ऋकारान्त in any gender, or is an ईकारान्त or ऊकारान्त स्त्रीलिङ्ग word	ईश्वरकर्तृकः	ईश्वरः कर्ता यस्य सः (ऋकारान्त पु.)
	सुशीलमातृकः	सुशीला माता यस्य सः (ऋकारान्त स्त्री.)
	अन्नधातृकः	अन्नं धातृ यस्य सः (ऋकारान्त नपु.)

(d) प्रादि Bahuvrihi – We have seen there are 22 avyayas belonging to [18] the group called प्रादयः। These can form the first words of a bahuvrihi under some situations. Resultant is a प्रादि बहुव्रीहिः।

→ Here the प्रादयः will be an उपसर्ग to a dhatu. To that a कृत् प्रत्यय will be added to form a कृदन्त verb. Then the कृदन्त will combine with another word to form a regular bahuvrihi. Then the धातु + कृत् प्रत्यय will be dropped and only the प्रादि will remain as the 1st word. This is a प्रादि bahuvrihi

eg निर् गता = दया यस्मात् सः → निर्गतादयः → निर्दयः
regular bahuvrihi प्रादि bahuvrihi

दुर् गता = बुद्धिः यस्य सः → दुर्गताबुद्धिः → दुर्बुद्धिः

eg शोभना बुद्धिः यस्य सः → सुबुद्धिः

	सुन्दरवधूकः	सुन्दरी वधूः यस्य सः (ऊकारान्त स्त्रीलिङ्ग)
	रूपवत्स्त्रीकः	रूपवती स्त्री यस्य सः (ईकारान्त स्त्रीलिङ्ग)

6. अलुक् समासः।

In cases where the विभक्ति remains in the समस्तपदम् , अलुक् समासः is seen. It can be any of the ones that we have studied in detail.

समस्तपदम्	विग्रहः	
युधिष्ठिरः	युधि स्थिरः	सप्तमीतत्पुरुषः
दुरादागतः	दुरात् आगतः	पञ्चमीतत्पुरुषः
दास्याःपुत्रः	दास्याः पुत्रः	षष्ठीतत्पुरुषः
गेहेशूरः	गेहे शूरः	सप्तमीतत्पुरुषः
परस्मैपदम्	परस्मै पदम्	चतुर्थीतत्पुरुषः
आत्मनेपदम्	आत्मने पदम्	चतुर्थीतत्पुरुषः
कण्ठेकालः	कण्ठे कालः	व्यधिकरणबहुव्रीहि
वनेचरः	वने चरः	उपपदसमासः

Mon 10.2.2014

8. नञ्समासः।

नञ् तत्पुरुषः is formed with the negative particle नञ् as the first word. Being a तत्पुरुषः the samasa will be उत्तरपद-प्रधान।

Add an अ if it is followed by a व्यञ्जनम् and an अन् if followed by a स्वरः।

समस्तपदम्	विग्रहः	अर्थ
अधर्मः	न धर्मः	
असन्देहः	न सन्देहः	
अविघ्नः	न विघ्नः	
अनश्वः	न अश्वः	
अनागमनम्	न आगमनम्	
अनिच्छा	न इच्छा	

19

Rule1 In this, the पूर्वपदः is न (न्+अ). When compounding is done, the नकार of न is dropped. Therefore न धर्मः → न्अ धर्मः → अधर्मः.

न = न् अ → अ → अन्

If the उत्तरपदः begins with a vowel, the अ which remains after dropping the नकार gets a नकार augment following it! and becomes अन्. Hence न आत्मा → न् अ आत्मा → अन् आत्मा → अनात्मा. 45/49

Month17

Another samasa on the lines of नञ् is the कु-समासः
This is used in the sense of निन्दा. It is also a type of नित्य समासः
eg कु धर्मः → ~~कुधर्मः~~ अधर्मः ।
Here the avyaya कु is the first word, with meaning कुत्सितः = निन्दितः = blame worthy.

अविवादः	न विवादः	eg
अपटुः	न पटुः	
अनुपलब्धिः	न उपलब्धिः	कुत्सितः पुरुषः → कुपुरुषः
अपन्थाः / अपन्थम्	न पन्थाः	
अपुत्रः	अविद्यमानः पुत्रः यस्य सः	कुत्सितः बुद्धिः → कुबुद्धिः
अनपत्यः	अविद्यमानम् अपत्यं यस्य सः	
अपुत्रीकः	अविद्यमाना पुत्री यस्य सः	कुत्सितः तार्किकः → कुतार्किकः
अप्रजाः	अविद्यमानः प्रजा यस्य सः	
अमेधाः	अविद्यमाना मेधा यस्य सः	
असहायः	न विद्यते सहायः यस्य सः	
अनपत्या	न विद्यते अपत्यं यस्याः सा	
अनृणः	न अस्ति ऋणं यस्य सः	

9. उपपदसमासः

This is a समासः with उपपदs. Here the word उपपद stands for any noun.

समस्तपदम्	विग्रहः	अर्थ
कुम्भकारः	कुम्भं करोति इति	
निशाकरः	निशां करोति इति	
तुन्दपरिमृजः	तुन्दं परिमार्ष्टि इति	
उष्णभोजी	उष्णं भुङ्क्ते इति	
सोमयाजी	सोमेन इष्टवान् इति	
शास्त्रकृत् / शास्त्रकारः	शास्त्रं करोति इति	
भाष्यकृत् / भाष्यकारः	भाष्यं करोति इति	
प्रियंवदः	प्रियं वदति इति	

Note : नित्य samasa : 4TP :- अस्वपदविग्रहवाक्यः

Generally when we compound a word, the पूर्वपदः and the उत्तरपदः 20 will be the same in the vigraha vakya, and the compound. This kind of Vigraha vakya is called स्वपदः विग्रह-वाक्यः.

But, in a नित्यसमासः either the पूर्वपदः or the उत्तरपदः will not be present. In place of the absent पूर्व/उत्तर पदः another word will be present in the compound! The विग्रह वाक्य of this compound is called अस्वपदविग्रहवाक्यः ।

Here, the word कृ happens to be नित्यम् as the first word whereas the second word can keep changing. Hence the sense of 'permanence'! And the vigrahavakya is an अस्वपद विग्रह वाक्यः ।

भयङ्करः	भयं करोति इति	
वंशवदः	वंशं वदति इति	
अभयङ्करः	अभयं करोति इति	
धनदः	धनं ददाति इति	
सामगः	साम गायति इति	
पण्डितंमन्यः/ पण्डितंमानी	पण्डितम् (आत्मानं) मन्यते इति ।	

Worksheets.

Just try and understand this:

समास भगवद्गीता द्वादशोध्यायः

एवं सततयुक्ता ये भक्तास्त्वां पर्युपासते ।
ये चाप्यक्षरमव्यक्तं तेषां के योगवित्तमाः ॥ १ ॥

१) न क्षरम् - अक्षरम् । (नञ् तत्पुरुष)

२) न व्यक्तम् - अव्यक्तम् । (नञ् तत्पुरुष)

३) योगे वित्तमाः - योगवित्तमाः । (सप्तमी तत्पुरुष)

सन्नियम्येन्द्रियग्रामं सर्वत्र समबुद्धयः ।
ते प्राप्नुवन्ति मामेव सर्वभूतहिते रताः ॥ ४ ॥

१) समा बुद्धिः येषां ते - समबुद्धयः । (बहुव्रीहि)

२) सर्वेभ्यः हितम् - सर्वहितम्, तस्मिन् - सर्वभूतहिते । (चतुर्थी तत्पुरुष)

अथैतदप्यशक्तोऽसि कर्तुं मद्योगमाश्रितः ।
सर्वकर्मफलत्यागं ततः कुरु यतात्मवान् ॥ ११ ॥

१) मम योगम् मद्योगम् । (षष्ठी तत्पुरुष)

मद्योगम् आश्रितः मद्योगमाश्रितः । (द्वितीया तत्पुरुष)

२) सर्वाणि कर्माणि - सर्वकर्माणि । (कर्मधारय) ब्राह्मणार्थं

In the 4TP example ब्राह्मणाय अन्नम् → the word अन्नम् is the उत्तरपदः in the वाक्यम् but is absent in the compound. Similarly the word अर्थः is the उत्तरपदः in the compound but not seen in the वाक्यम्.

So we say, the word अर्थ is permanently in the compound, hence the name नित्य samasa!

चतुर्थ्यन्तं पदम् अर्थेन सह नित्यम् समस्यते

47/49
Month 17

सर्वकर्मणां फलानि - सर्वकर्मफलानि । (षष्ठी तत्पुरुष)
सर्वकर्मफलानां त्यागः - सर्वकर्मफलत्यागः, तम् - सर्वकर्मफलत्यागम् । (षष्ठी तत्पुरुष)

अद्वेष्टा सर्वभूतानां मैत्रः करुण एव च ।
निर्ममो निरहङ्कारः समदुःखसुखः क्षमी ॥ १३ ॥
१) सर्वे भूताः - सर्वभूताः, तेषाम् - सर्वभूतानाम् । (कर्मधारय)
२) निगतं ममत्वं यस्मात् सः - निर्ममः । (प्रादि बहुव्रीहि)
३) निर्गतः अहङ्कारः यस्मात् सः - निरहङ्कारः । (प्रादि बहुव्रीहि)
४) दुःखं च सुखं च – दुःखसुखे । (द्वन्द्व)
समः दुःखसुखयोः यः सः - समदुःखसुखः । (बहुव्रीहि)

सन्तुष्टः सततं योगी यतात्मा दृढनिश्चयः ।
मय्यर्पितमनोबुद्धिर्यो मद्भक्तः स मे प्रियः ॥ १४ ॥
१) दृढः निश्चयः - दृढनिश्चयः । (कर्मधारय)
दृढनिश्चयः यस्य सः - दृढनिश्चयः । (बहुव्रीहि)
२) मनः च बुद्धिः - मनोबुद्धी । (द्वन्द्व)
अर्पितं मनोबुद्धी येन सः - अर्पितमनोबुद्धिः । (बहुव्रीहि)

यस्मान्नोद्विजते लोको लोकान्नोद्विजते च यः ।
हर्षामर्षभयोद्वेगैर्मुक्तो यः स च मे प्रियः ॥ १५ ॥
१) हर्षः च अमर्षः च भयं च उद्वेगः च - हर्षामर्षभयोद्वेगाः । (द्वन्द्व)
हर्षामर्षभयोद्वेगैः मुक्तः यः सः - हर्षामर्षभयोद्वेगैर्मुक्ताः । (बहुव्रीहि)

अनपेक्षः शुचिर्दक्ष उदासीनो गतव्यथः ।
सर्वारम्भपरित्यागी यो मद्भक्तः स मे प्रियः ॥ १६ ॥
१) न विद्यते अपेक्षा यस्मिन् सः - अनपेक्षः । (बहुव्रीहि)
२) गता व्यथा यस्मात् सः - गतव्यथः । (बहुव्रीहि)

यो न हृष्यति न द्वेष्टि न शोचति न काङ्क्षति ।

the 22 upasargas (Dhatuvrpmanjari pg 6)
22

प्रादि तत्पुरुषः

Rule A group of अव्ययs called as प्रादयः (प्र, etc) will combine with a meaningfully related word to form a प्रादितत्पुरुषः समासः ।

These are also नित्य समासs ।

शुभाशुभपरित्यागी भक्तिमान्य: स मे प्रिय: ॥ १७ ॥

१) शुभं च अशुभं च – शुभाशुभे । (द्वन्द्व)

शुभाशुभयो: परित्यागी य: स: - शुभाशुभपरित्यागी । (बहुव्रीहि)

सम: शत्रौ च मित्रे च तथा मानापमानयो: ।

शीतोष्णसुखदु:खेषु सम: सङ्गविवर्जित: ॥ १८ ॥

१) मान: च अपमान: च – मानापमानौ, तयो: - मानापमानयो: । (द्वन्द्व)

२) शीतं च उष्णं च सुखं च दु:खं च - शीतोष्णसुखदु:खानि, तेषु - शीतोष्णसुखदु:खेषु । (द्वन्द्व)

३) सङ्गं विवर्जितं येन स: - सङ्गविवर्जित: । (बहुव्रीहि)

तुल्यनिन्दास्तुतिर्मौनी सन्तुष्टो येन केनचित् ।

अनिकेत: स्थिरमतिर्भक्तिमान्मे प्रियो नर: ॥ १९ ॥

१) स्थिरा मति: यस्य स: - स्थिरमति: । (बहुव्रीहि)

***

Please do write in case you have any questions regarding this lesson. Hesitate not and thy doubts shall be gone with the wind! 20.2.2014 Thu. षष्ठी

upasargas = The प्रादि group of avyayas can form ① प्रादि तत्पुरुष: ② प्रादि बहुव्रीहि and ③ अव्ययी भाव: compounds.

The प्रादि तत्पुरुष is a नित्य samasa, therefore will have अस्वपदविग्रह:

eg शोभन: पुरुष: → सुपुरुष: , 'शोभन' is substituted by 'सु', ∴ नित्यसमास:

शोभन: जन: → सुजन:

दुराचार: पुरुष: → दुष्पुरुष:

प्रगत: आचार्य: → प्राचार्य: = retired teacher; here प्र upasarga means गत: past participle passive

अभि = गत: मुखम् → अभिमुखम् = in front of (someone)

प्रति = गत: अक्षम् → प्रत्यक्षम् [अक्षम् अक्षम् प्रति] = direct perception

उपपदतत्पुरुष: = सोपपदकृत् (Panini Ch 3.2)

This is a kind of samasa which comes in the section of तत्पुरुष: samasa and in the section of कृदन्त: ।
Here the कृदन्त: formation and the samasa formation are intrinsically together.

23

49/44 Month 17

In fact, the कृदन्तः will form only when an उपपदः is present. And the कृदन्तः pratipadika which is formed, will combine with the उपपदः, without becoming a padam first.

We have seen samasa will take place only between 2 padas. In that sense, this is an exception. The pratipadika will combine with an uppada. and

eg कुम्भं करोति इति । vigraha vakya

→ कुम्भं + (कृ + अण्) (Here अण् denotes the कर्ता)

Remember the rule that णिच् in 10_c causes Vriddhi of root vowel

Remember that सार्वधातुकम् are those that have तिङ् or शत् प्रत्ययs ।

Here the प्रत्यय is कृदन्तः, so it is आर्धधातुकम् ।

→ कुम्भम् + (क् आर् अण्) Vriddhi substitution

→ कुम्भम् + (कार् + अ) the ण् is इत् letter and after doing the Vriddhi it dropped

→ कुम्भम् + कार → कुम्भकार (m) pratipadika → कुम्भकारः (m1/1)
(it gives rise to a pratipadika)

eg सूत्रम् (2/1) करोति इति सूत्रकारः

भाष्यम् (2/1) करोति इति भाष्यकारः

भयम् (2/1) करोति इति भयङ्करः

सोमेन (3/1) इष्टवान् इति सोमयाजी (सोमेन + (यज् + णिनि)

Note: उपपदतत्पुरुषः is a नित्यसमासः ।

उष्णम् भुङ्क्तुं शीलम् अस्य → उष्णम् + (भुज् + णिनि) → उष्णभोजिन् (m)

The one who ~~also~~ has the nature of eating hot → ~~उष्णभोजि~~ → उष्णभोजी (m1/1)

ब्रह्म चरितुम् शीलम् अस्य → ब्रह्मचारी

→ ब्रह्म + (चर + णिनि) → ब्रह्मचारिन् (m) → ब्रह्मचारी (m1/1)

Similarly, Bhagavad Gita → अमृतवर्षिणी (f1/1) → ब्रह्मचारिणी (f1/1)

latter, two words are placed side by side (without the need for a सन्धिः to take place) to form a single word.

In a समासः , the समस्तपद is the compound word... देवदासः । विग्रह is when you break it up into its components..... देवस्य दासः । i.e. any compound can be written as its original sentence, known as विग्रहः .

Naturally, it is with time that you will figure out in which combinations these work out, for example दासदेवः would not be correct. And it is with time that you will figure out which words can be made a समास of. For example, वनप्राप्तः is allowed and NOT वनप्राप्तवान् । Not to worry. In this case at least ...Time will wait for the Sanskrit enthusiast!

> **Note:**
>
> This lesson is to help you figure out what समास words mean whenever you come across them in your course of reading. You also now have the wherewithal to form your own combination words intelligently.
> Another thing to remember is that people are all made differently. Many a time you will find that someone may have formed a समास in one way and you may prefer another. Both may be correct. So just relax and enjoy learning something new.

समास can be divided into 6 classes according to the sense that they convey when dissolved.

द्वन्द्वो द्विगुरपि चाहं मद्गेहे नित्यमव्ययीभावः ।
तत्पुरुष कर्मधारय येनाहं स्यां बहुव्रीहिः ॥

For our convenience, I have divided them into 9 groups. I have been better able to retain the information with a wider classification like that.

समासः

Def :- When two subantam padams that are meaningfully connected in such a way they can be combined to give a unified meaning, are combined it is called the process of compounding. 2

Here, the process is called समासः
and the result is also called समासः

Process of Compounding = समासः समासनम्

The combined word is called a समासः
(समासः That which is combined = कर्म-व्युत्पत्तिः)

Maheshwar Sutras and Pratyaharas

माहेश्वराणि सूत्राणि are sounds that are a rearrangement of the Devanagari Alphabet for grammatical use. Listed at the start of the Ashtadhyayi Sutrapatha. Consonants have been written with अकार solely for enunciation. But the लँण् = ल् अँ ण् contains लकार, anunasika Tag अँ, and consonant Tag ण् ।

SN	Maheshwar Sutras		Pratyahara	Count
1	अइउण्	All vowels = अच्	अण्	1
2	ऋऌक्	Simple vowels = अक्	अक् इक् उक्	3
3	एओङ्	Diphthongs = एच्	एङ्	1
4	ऐऔच्	Semivowels = यण्	अच् इच् एच् ऐच्	4
5	हयवरट्	All consonants = हल्	अट्	1
6	लँण्	ल्+अँ, No nasal for र्	अण् इण् यण् रँ	3
7	ञमङणनम्	5th of row = Nasals = ञम्	अम् यम् ङम् ञम्	3
8	झभञ्	4th of row = झष्	यञ्	1
9	घढधष्	are all soft consonants	झष् भष्	2
10	जबगडदश्	3rd of row = जश् (soft)	अश् हश् वश् झश् जश् बश्	6
11	खफछठथचटतव्	1st and 2nd of row = खय् are all hard consonants	छव् खँ	1
12	कपय्		यय् मय् झय् खय् चय् ञय्	4
13	शषसर्	Sibilants (hard) = शर्	यर् झर् खर् चर् शर्	5
14	हल्	Aspirate is soft	अल् हल् वल् रल् झल् शल्	6
			Basic Count of Pratyaharas =	41
			Extended Count 41 + 3 = 44 + 2 with later grammarians =	46

Epilogue

Compound words are frequently seen in Sanskrit Vedanta and Upanishad texts. These are condensed sentences, nay entire paragraphs of subtle wisdom.

सर्वे भवन्तु सुखिनः । सर्वे सन्तु निरामयाः ।
सर्वे भद्राणि पश्यन्तु । मा कश्चिद् दुःख भाग् भवेत् ॥
ॐ शान्तिः शान्तिः शान्तिः ॥

When faith has blossomed in life, Every step is led by the Divine.

Sri Ravi Shankar

Om Namah Shivaya

जय गुरुदेव

www.ingramcontent.com/pod-product-compliance
Ingram Content Group UK Ltd.
Pitfield, Milton Keynes, MK11 3LW, UK
UKHW061540190726
13845UKWH00031B/1139

9 789395 766913